Mississippi Born—California Bound

How Jim Crow and Racism Lost to a Family Legacy

Eugene Spencer, Jr., DDS

Mississippi Born—California Bound: How Jim Crow and Racism Lost to a Family Legacy

Published in the United States of America

Sunshine Solutions Publishing
9912 Business Park Dr., Ste. 170
Sacramento, CA 95827

Library of Congress Control Number   2018958644

ISBN-13: 978-1727406450
ISBN-10: 1727406451

Dedication

I would not be who I am today without my parents, Reverend Eugene Emmett Spencer and Mrs. Pauline Young Spencer. Daddy, you taught me by example how to be a strong man, dedicated and committed to my family. Mother Dear, you taught me how to be loving and compassionate. You set boundaries and kept me focused on my studies.

Thank you both for giving me a solid foundation to traverse my life's journey with triumph. I have such admiration for your fortitude and your accomplishments will dwell in my heart, in tribute to you.

You taught me that God is first always, and with family everything is possible and achievable. You taught me to walk in love, to develop a strong work ethic, to always remember to serve my community, and to share my blessings.

You taught me that no one will ever take my education away from me. You taught me to invest wisely, work hard, and be masterful when choosing my inner circle. I love you both so much and look forward to seeing you again.

To my wife and life partner of 55 years, Maude Walters Spencer, I love you so very much. I know that you have always been attached to my life's journey. You are inseparable from my expressions and experiences. You were instrumental in helping me produce this historical document. Your advice and counsel keep me grounded and grateful for each new day. Thank you for loving me. Thank you for your gift of true partnership. Thank you for your sacrifices to our family. I will love you to the end.

4

Acknowledgments

To my only living sibling, Doris, thank you for your encouragement to write my life's history. I would never have completed this without your assistance in researching family information and history. You have been an invaluable asset. I know that we both share deep love and honor to our siblings who have preceded us in death. Rosia, Harold, and Delano, your spirits are heartfelt.

To Maude (BA, MS): thanks for being an ambassador of higher education for our children. To Gena Spencer Middleton (BA, MA, DACM): thank you for pursuing your dreams and serving your community. To my daughter-in-law, Janet Castellanos Spencer (BA): thank you for your educational accomplishments and steadfast example of excellence. To Brian Spencer (BA): thank you for your strength and your adventurous spirit. I am so proud of your community activism. To Arika Spencer-Brown (MBA, EdD), Liaison with Peralta Colleges at the Oakland Military Institute, in Oakland, CA: you are carrying on the family legacy of education. This means so much to me. And thanks to Jennifer Spencer Duncan (BA, MS), senior sales proposal specialist with Blue Shield Insurance: thank you for continuing our legacy of education. I am so very proud of each of you. Thank you for exceeding my expectations. Thank you for living according to the Golden Rule. To my sons-in-law, Glenn Middleton (DDS), Robert Brown (MBA), and Darren Duncan (MBA): kudos to each of you for your dedicated accomplishments and contributions.

To Dr. and Mrs. Roscoe Brewer: your everlasting concern, words and advice, will be cherished and appreciated by me. Your thoughts strengthen my perseverance. To Patrick Melarkley (DDS): your assistance in aiding me to launch my practice in the days of discrimination served as a beacon of hope to survive in a racist society. Thanks for your courage and comfort.

To my daughter-in-law Janet and my grandson Brian for scanning all of the pictures for this project. To Harrison for his interest and encouragement in my writing this book.

Table of Contents

Introduction

There is so much going on in the world today that disheartens me. Many African-American families and communities are currently under attack from all sides. The generational lineage, where grandparents, parents, and children often grew up under one roof, are long gone. Single-parent homes have left holes in the souls of our youngsters that will never be filled.

I grew up with my parents, my maternal grandmother, aunts and uncles who were always available to communicate, guide, control, and console me. I was raised when the elders led by example. We may have been economically poor, but we were never lacking love and support.

I was taught values and held accountable to live up to them. I was not allowed to not serve God and community. I raised my family on those same principles and want my children and grandchildren to understand what I went through and how to live in gratitude.

I offer this journey of love to my wife, children, and grandchildren; to all those who do not have loving families; and to those who are in the midst of turmoil, as evidence that all things are possible. Every one of us has the potential. Every problem has a solution and every excuse is equal. I believe that no one can take your education away from you.

1   Growing Up in the Rural South

I was born in the country, just outside the small town of Port Gibson in Claiborne County, Mississippi. Port Gibson was first settled by French colonists just over two hundred years before my birth (1729) and chartered as a town after the Louisiana Purchase in 1803. Many Native American tribes lived on these lands. The French colonists, however, pushed the Native Americans from their land. This was known as the Indian Removal, whereby the United States government, in the 19th century, forcibly removed Native Americans from their ancestral homelands in the eastern United States to the lands west of the Mississippi River.

Large cotton plantations were developed on the lands once the Native Americans were driven out, and farmers in the state imported thousands of Negro slaves from the Upper South to work on the new plantations. Claiborne County had a Negro majority established well before the Civil War (1861–1865) who were disturbingly enslaved. In 1863, while crossing the Mississippi River in his quest to capture Vicksburg, General Grant came upon Port Gibson and ordered that the town be spared because it was too beautiful to burn. It was saved, oddly, due to the grandeur and expanse of those antebellum mansions and plantations.

In the late 1920s and early 1930s, not much had changed. These antebellum plantations continued the very institutions of slavery, which led to an economic ideology that exacerbated the social and economic patterns of the South. With a population of nearly 1,700 people, White landowners reaped large profits from cotton production, with Negro tenant farmers working the land. My father, Reverend Eugene E. Spencer, was a country preacher. He and my mother, Pauline E. M. Spencer, were sharecroppers who worked on one of the large cotton plantations.

The White landlords popularized sharecropping by agreeing that the Negro tenant farmer would farm the land in return for a share in the profits, usually at the end of the farm season. However, the system was certainly self-defeating economically for the Negro sharecroppers because they were exploited by the merchant farmers. My parents were smart enough to know that it would be an uphill battle to leave the plantation. They knew in their hearts that this situation would never be the final narrative for them.

Although many landlords pretended to foster a cozy relationship with the Negro tenant farmers, my parents were not easily deceived. The landlords did all they could to make sure the system guaranteed that those like my parents were constantly behind in paying their debt, forbidding them to escape poverty. It was the landlords' intention to maintain control, treating the tenant farmers as chattel slaves, as if they were actual articles of the property, using intimidation tactics to remind the tenant farmers of days not long past when they truly were "colored" and subject to physical harm.

These mental mind games cemented tenant farmers' perpetual indebtedness to landlords year after year. The end result was an economic bondage to the landlord's land for entire Negro families. But not ours. My father lived the Word of God that he preached. He knew in his spirit that there was a way out of this. He and my mother were strong in their resolve to learn everything they could about sharecropping.

Landlords generated high interest rates for loans, supplies, seed, fertilizer, food, and leased equipment, while requiring 50% of farm production. They manipulated the balances by adding the principle from the *current* year to the carryover from the *prior* year. Knowing that the carryover from the prior year had already been taxed once was of no consequence to the landlord, yet it was a huge consequence for the tenant farmers. The entire total was then taxed again and again, at high interest rates, year after year.

My father and mother knew that the calculations were corrupt and dishonest. The White landlords underestimated the power of Negro families working together for the good of their entire community. Negro families were neither docile nor submissive. They developed an independent culture and unspoken language, single-minded in their approach to finding a way out and betterment for all. To provide a better life for my parents and their family, my father knew that they had to work harder in order to reach his goal of one day owning his own farm. My mother gave her full support. They lived what they were trying to accomplish: a true partnership and team, not limited by someone else's defined roles for their success, but created from their own sheer grit and determination to provide more for their family.

We moved to this part of Mississippi because my father became the pastor of Mercy Seat Missionary Baptist Church. He was called to preach, delivering the gospel to his people. God chose a good and faithful servant. My father was built to carry the weight of the community on his broad shoulders. He was tall, fair-skinned, and clean-shaven. He walked with a dignity and respect second to none. He was held in high regard among his peers because he treated them with the respect and reverence they deserved.

My mother was well-suited for my father. Although he was seven years her senior, she paired her sensibility and trust with his determination and vision. They loved each other. Her thin, 5'4"-frame complimented his. Her medium-brown skin glowed in the sunlight. Her brown eyes twinkled when she smiled. She was strong and very knowledgeable.

I was born at the end of January in 1932. In those days, while Mississippi winters were moderately cool when the sun was up, after the evening sun had set the temperatures would drop down to almost 30 degrees. My father worked from dawn to dusk in the fields, so my mother made their home as comfortable as she could. It wasn't easy during normal times, but all of the wives in the community worked as best they could, sharing what they had on hand with each other. I was delivered by a midwife in the confines of that small shack they had leased from the landlord.

Negro midwives were also part of the community, and knew the mother's history, breastfeeding ability, and even whether she would be strong enough to carry a baby to term. They were spiritual healers with rich traditions of their own, passed down from their grandmothers and mothers. They watched over the Negro mothers during the entire pregnancy, especially if something was wrong or not progressing normally. Midwives were hampered by the same socioeconomic barriers of the times, but they used ancestral traditions and rituals to safely aid the mothers through childbirth.

Most of the births occurred in the homes because there were not very many hospitals to begin with, and none of them allowed access for Negroes. Mississippi had the highest maternal death rate and the highest infant mortality rate of the entire United States. Miss Janie Breckenridge was the best midwife in our community and my parents had great respect for her. They described her as a savior with the spiritual guidance and gift from God to aid in the many deliveries. When it was time, my father sent for her.

Miss Janie came and got my parents' room ready for the birthing process, preparing herbs and teas to help my mother relax. My father brought water in from the well and heated it while Miss Janie gathered rags and towels she would need for my mother. Then they waited. My father was in the other room. Miss Janie was with my mother. When the time came, Miss Janie delivered me, cleaned me up, and swatted my buttocks so that Mother could hear my voice for the first time and know that I was healthy. Miss Janie introduced me to who I would come to know and love as "Mother Dear." That same day, my father, who was patiently waiting in the adjacent room, became my "Daddy." I was

14

named after him. Mother Dear nursed me, fed me, and loved me with all of her heart. I had Daddy's skin color and Mother Dear's gentle smile.

Mother Dear spent the next few weeks getting used to being a new mother and dealing with the aftermath of childbirth. At the same time, she knew she needed to return to the fields.

Time passed, and things got back to normal for Mother Dear. Our family continued to grow. A year after I was born, Rosia came. The next year, my brother Harold was born and once again, Miss Janie came to Mother Dear's rescue. Then, Delano, my youngest brother came. Miss Janie came to help Mother Dear whenever she got pregnant. By the time Delano was born, I was old enough to know that I did not like it when Mother Dear was in pain. Miss Janie stayed with Mother Dear for a long time as she screamed and called out for help. I was in the adjacent room and attempted to go in the room with her, but Daddy and Miss Janie restrained me. I felt helpless and could not tolerate hearing Mother Dear suffer from such severe pain.

My sister Doris was born, two years after Delano, in 1938. Once again, Janie and Daddy had to restrain me from getting to Mother Dear, certain that my presence would not ease her pain. I was relieved after the birth of my little sister and I immediately went into the room to cuddle Mother Dear. I was happy to see Doris. After about six weeks, Mother Dear resumed her usual responsibilities.

Our parents continued to work on the farm as dedicated sharecroppers, providing the necessary benefits for us children. They were humble in their unerring work, determined to provide love, character, and confidence as the foundation for our family. Mother Dear focused on the demands of the family. Daddy increased his work in the fields as more children were being born, focusing on the demands of the farm and learning as much as he could.

Cotton was the mainstay of farm products, and my parents farmed practically the whole year harvesting cotton, soy beans, peanuts, oats, watermelons, maize, potatoes, hay, and tomatoes for income and consumption. Mother Dear made sure Daddy had a clean shirt and overalls for the long days in the fields. He rose early every morning and was dressed in time to grab a bite to eat and be in the fields by 7:00 a.m.

Fieldwork was hard. The Mississippi summer was hot and humid. The sun beat down on you until your exposed skin was a shade or two darker than your skin underneath the overalls. Daddy carried an old rag in his back pocket to wipe the sweat from his brow. His hands were rugged and calloused. He used every farming tool on the property. He had the strength and analytical prowess to ensure each row was calculated to precise measurements. Any errors could result in the loss of crop, leading to a financial loss for our family. Each row needed adequate room to grow the crops. Daddy tilled the soil, planted the seeds, and watched as each new sprout gently broke ground. He tended his parcel of the landlord's land as if he owned it.

Each day around 11:00 a.m., Mother Dear would prepare lunch from whatever was available in the season. It was good to spend time with Daddy for a short recess from his back-breaking work in the fields. We all ate under the shade of a tree. Then, Mother Dear would gather up the pots and utensils, and we walked back to our little shack while Daddy returned to the fieldwork. He wouldn't return home until after 6:00 p.m.

2 The Pastor

Daddy was not only a sharecropper; he was the Pastor of the Mercy Seat Missionary Baptist Church. Both of our parents were saintly and attended church services with a passion. Daddy preached all over the state and administrated spiritual needs to the membership. Many of the Negro citizens were very poor. They were trapped in poverty with health problems and lacked any visions of success, acclimated to the racist depictions of their Negro race. They were often disrespected and mistreated and called "Niggers" by the Whites.

Daddy preached in revivals throughout Southwest Mississippi. Usually, a church revival would last a week and he preached each night to "save the sinners." This was quite a religious ordeal in Negro communities. This was a time of spiritual rejoicing, happiness, and of praising God. Daddy would tell Mother Dear all about it. He said he felt freedom, forgiveness, and love when connecting with others, young and old, sharing, and creating lasting friendships. At the end of the revival week, the members would bring food in horse-driven wagons to the church. The food served included exotic desserts of potato pies, custards, pound cakes, chocolate cakes, coconut cakes, lemon cakes, pecan pies, blackberry pies, lemon meringue pies, ice cream, and fruit cakes. Chicken, pork, beef, lamb, and sausage were in abundance. It seemed every imaginable vegetable was available and seasoned with ham hocks.

Many of the female members worked daily in the kitchens owned by their White masters and prepared food in the same kitchen to be carried to the church. Some members took produce from the master's home. The members ate without any regard to their health. This was a joyous occasion to celebrate with friends, relatives, the poor, and all that wanted to be blessed by the "Heavenly Father." These blessings were not only a spiritual value to strengthen their belief in God, but also provided social media for our people.

The church was the center of Negro culture and it was the only place for them to congregate without being harassed or intimidated by Whites. The Ku Klux Klan and other White hate groups burned or destroyed Negro churches during the evenings. The gatherings at the church were an expression of love, freedom, and faith for the people. It was a beautiful scene to see the many enthusiastic people who were otherwise oppressed daily in the normal pursuit of justice.

Mother Dear always listened attentively when Daddy returned home from the revivals. She knew that Daddy was so busy each day delivering his sermons, and she was happy to hear about all that went on while he was away. We missed him, too. He always took a little time to play with us while he was talking with Mother Dear.

When Daddy was not traveling, we attended church with him on Sunday mornings at Mercy Seat Missionary Baptist Church. There was plenty of family nearby including uncles, aunts, cousins, and my favorite grandmother. Sundays were unofficially declared a day for us to have dinner with my "Big Mama." She was Mother Dear's mother, Mary Jane Young. Big Mama lived in a neat two-bedroom cottage behind a home owned by Henry Galloway. Henry Galloway was my grandmother's master. Henry Galloway and his wife allowed my grandmother to prepare scrumptious meals on late Sunday afternoons for our family. She was a great cook and prepared many dishes for this gathering. We could not enter the front door of the Galloway home. It was mandatory for Negroes to only enter a White person's home through the back door.

Nevertheless, after entry, we were permitted to peruse around. It was breathtaking to observe the home furnishings and niceties displayed in an antebellum southern colonial home. Our family would visit Big Mama's cottage first, if only for a few minutes to follow protocol, and then enter through the back door of the Galloway home. I was in awe each time I visited the home, comparing Big Mama's shack to our home and living conditions.

It was customary to have our meal in the formal dining room. Big Mama would have the dining room and table beautifully decorated in a formal setting. There was a very large crystal chandelier hanging over the dining table with a full set of sterling silverware and fine china dinnerware. During our dinner, the Galloways would come and go from the dining room, checking to see if we were enjoying the meal and chatting briefly. I do believe they were sincere about having us over for the meal. I think Mrs. Galloway loved having children in her home. They were cautious about their neighbors knowing that we were visiting their home, though. As soon as we finished the meal, Big

Mama escorted us back to her quaint little cottage.

After we left her, Big Mama would soon return to her master's residence and perform her routine cleaning chores with zeal and compassion. Daddy and Mother Dear understood her dedication and loyalty to the Galloways. They knew that Big Mama's ability to have us dine in the Galloways' home was a reflection of her core values and how much the Galloways respected her. Daddy and Mother Dear also knew that it was necessary to teach us how important it was for all of us to act differently when we were in that home. It was also necessary that all of us understand the importance of not doing anything to compromise Big Mama's good fortune.

This was routine for our family on Sundays after church service.

We usually stayed until dusk because Mother Dear did not want to leave Big Mama alone. We were sad to leave her after such a loving visit, too. On occasion, Mother Dear would shed a tear. As we visited our grandmother, I inquired about our grandfather and was told to "keep my mouth shut" by Mother Dear. This seemed to be off limits for discussion and did not sit well with me. I grappled with it from time to time and wondered if my grandfather was safe, hoping one day to meet him.

Big Mama never spoke of our grandfather. She was soft-spoken and kind, with a thick frame and arms that were just the right length to hold us tight. We snuggled with her while she administered enough hugs and kisses to make each of us want more. We always made sure she knew how much we loved her. She allowed us to sneak over to get some ice cream while she was cleaning and scrubbing the Galloways' home sometimes.

On other Sundays, our family would make a second visit to our aunt's home, Mother Dear's sister. During these visits, Aunt Sis would insist that we have dessert as either a treat or a full meal. We always enjoyed our time with her. She liked to tickle us so that she could hear us laugh.

Finally, the family would depart for evening church services. These sequences of events occurred regularly. Daddy was a pastor at four churches. He preached every Sunday, alternating between the churches and accompanied by our entire family. We attended services practically all day because we had Sunday school at 9:00 a.m. followed by regular service from 10:00 a.m. to 2:00 p.m. Daddy also insisted that we attend the Baptist Training Union sessions at 6:00 p.m. We arrived at home between 8:00 p.m. and 9:00 p.m. and finally settled in bed around 9:30 p.m. This schedule was very strenuous and challenging for all of us, but I never heard either Daddy or Mother Dear complain.

3 Time for School

Summer was over, and it was time for all of the children in the community to go back to school. Elementary schools for Negroes throughout Claiborne County were either located inside the churches or on the church grounds. Mercy Seat Missionary Baptist Church had two rooms in the back of the building that were used for the elementary school. Each room was separated into four classrooms by thin partitions. First grade through fourth grade were in one room and fifth grade through eighth grade were in the other room.

It was unlawful to admit a Negro student in school before age six in Mississippi. School started in September, so I was still age five. I wouldn't turn six until the following January. I really wanted to go to school because Daddy and Mother Dear talked about education all the time. I was excited about being the first one in school. They were able to convince the principal to allow me to begin school early. If the White Superintendent of Education had been aware of this, I would have been expelled from school and the Negro Principal would have been placed on probation or terminated. Quite naturally, both my parents constantly reminded me not to speak to anyone about this. I did not want to do anything to disappoint them, so I did as they instructed.

Many Negro teachers, high school principals, and college professors risked being placed on probation or terminated for not sacrificing their moral beliefs. It was a common occurrence for them to hide the real truths for the good of the children. Hatred and anger of White

Mississippi residents smoldered beneath the surface, which ultimately gave rise to the lynchings and killings of Negroes, as well as denying them access to an education. The few schools for Negroes ascribed to the racist Jim Crow laws.

On school days, I walked about two miles to school escorted by older students. I was happy to be in school, but my first-grade teacher, Mrs. Shaffer, was very strict and I thought she was a mean person. She was dedicated to her profession and had to be clear with her students that there was a structure to learning that required discipline and practice. I felt that she was really demanding. I did not quite understand why she sent notes to my parents regularly showing my progress in class. She drilled us in math and reading for county competitions against other Negro schools. Mrs. Shaffer truly brought the level best out of us. She always encouraged her students to lead and demonstrate the highest degree of character among the other students.

Once I got a little more comfortable in her class, I realized that Mrs. Shaffer was an excellent teacher with high moral standards. Since our first-grade class shared the room with three other grades, each teacher required strict discipline in their classrooms. The other teachers went along with Mrs. Shaffer's vision, following the procedures she put in place for educating us children. The partition separating each class was a sliding board and made a loud screeching noise when opened and closed. The other classes could hear and observe Mrs. Shaffer, just as we could hear the assistant teachers teaching their classes. However, the students in each class were preoccupied with doing their own assignments and were a bit oblivious to the other classes.

Sometimes, the teacher assistants from the other grades taught our class while Mrs. Shaffer went to teach one of the higher grades. No matter which grade she was teaching, Mrs. Shaffer did not tolerate any student from another class interfering when she was teaching. Mrs. Shaffer ruled the school in Mercy Seat Missionary Baptist Church. She supervised all of the teaching methods for all of the grades. She was widely known as a notable teacher in Claiborne County.

One of her most outstanding traits as a teacher was the craftsmanship that she used to become a personal tutor for each student that needed extra help. Our teachers encouraged us to participate in the school's meager arts program, including the Thanksgiving and Christmas plays. Many of the students exhibited stage fright initially. However, through practicing over and over, wonderful Mrs. Shaffer developed students with the utmost confidence and pride. She instilled in each of us a thirst to reach for the mountaintop.

It was no secret that the White students in Port Gibson attended schools that were segregated from the "colored schools." The White students had excellent, modern buildings with heated rooms during the winter months. On many occasions, our elementary school was cold during the winter, which made it difficult to concentrate on our subjects. During the summer months, our windows and front doors were left open to have a breeze for comfort and relief from the heat and humidity. Also, our supplies and books were old hand-me-downs from the White schools with the pages marked up or missing altogether.

These inhumane conditions did not stop our courageous teachers. They instilled pride in us to excel in our studies and to persevere. Mrs. Shaffer was determined to give us confidence for the task of learning and our parents supported the programs. This was accomplished through meetings with our parents. Mrs. Shaffer demanded that one or both of our parents come to the school to be knowledgeable about our progress. On occasion, Mother Dear would attend the sessions without Daddy. Mother Dear prided herself on not missing a session because she wanted me to adhere to the standards. Daddy attended these sessions whenever he was available. Often, he was busy with church work or fieldwork. I had the utmost respect for both of them and did not question their love and dedication.

Daddy was an excellent family man with high moral standards. Mother Dear was a very proud and charismatic person with deep regrets about not working as hard as Daddy. Our family continued to strive for success, even though the system of sharecropping was extremely hard. My parents instilled in me at this young age to excel in school and strive to be a responsible person. They required me to complete all of my school work assignments before bed. Mother Dear reviewed my writing assignments and made sure that my writing was legible; if not, I had to redo it. She drilled me over and over for content and clarity.

Daddy was very particular about my math work. He was most concerned about me learning to solve the complicated math problems in the textbook. Nevertheless, he never knew that I was riling against his wishes and techniques in explaining the math problems, simply because I was passive and did not desire to concentrate in analyzing the problems. Even though the books were hand-me-downs from the White schools, he encouraged me to understand the problems, telling me "No one can take or destroy your knowledge," even during these days of evil segregation and discrimination in Mississippi. It seemed as though I could not hear him. I kept focusing on the fact that our books were in poor condition—they had pages missing and were the stained, soiled, and unreadable leftovers from the White schools. Daddy did not lose his patience. He simply repeated what he was trying to get me to understand. "Once you get knowledge of any kind, no one can ever take it away from you," he said.

Mrs. Shaffer must have understood the same thing. If one of the pages in one book was missing, she would cross reference it with another book that had that page. She was quite skillful; if a page was marked out or unreadable, she would ask the other classmates if they had the needed information in their books. This really developed a close relationship with our classmates and families because we shared and supported each other in our daily activities. Continuing tutoring in math with Daddy had its tense moments because he required that I understood the fundamentals of addition, subtraction, multiplication, and division early in elementary school.

I felt like it was extra important to him because he had to figure out how much cotton he picked, weigh it, and multiply how much money he should get back when he turned it in to the merchants. He had to divide up how much money belonged to the landlord and how much belonged to us. I knew that the more bales of cotton Daddy harvested, the more money he made for us. I knew that Mother Dear understood it also because every once in a while, she worked in the field alongside him.

Mother Dear had her hands full with me, Rosia, Harold, and our new baby brother, Delano, who arrived two years after Harold. With more mouths to feed, she and Daddy decided it was time to introduce me to picking cotton to help harvest the farm products daily. I was happy to help the family in any way I could. At age five, Daddy taught me how to bridle, feed, communicate with, and care for the livestock. On the farm, there were cattle, hogs, sheep, mules, and horses. Mules and horses were used to prepare the soil for planting and harvesting our crops. I arose at 5:00 a.m. with Daddy from Monday through Friday and worked the crops daily from 7:00 a.m. until it was time for school. On Saturdays, I worked the crops with Daddy from 7:00 a.m. to dusk.

As my other siblings became older, all of us would work in some capacity to increase the production of our farm. Harold and I worked in the field with Daddy while Rosia worked in the kitchen with Mother Dear helping to prepare the meals. At the end of the day, our evening meal was a welcome break from our daily chores. When that exhaustion set in, it limited all physical aspirations to do much playing around. We had a ritual before retiring for the evening to take a bath in a tin tub with heated water from the stove top and repeat the Lord's Prayer. Oh, how very well I slept through the night, as I was completely debilitated and weary from the daily farm work.

Daddy spent immeasurable time calculating his share of the net profits in meetings with the landlord or landowner. It was complicated because not only did the landlord demand 50% of net profits, he also charged a hefty interest rate for farm supplies on the advanced loans to Daddy. The landlord basically set his own interest rates to maximize his profits. Each year, Daddy would face this formula with a heavy heart. I could read my parents' frustrations and disappointments because they worked extremely hard to provide for the family. We were still poor, lacking clothing essentials, balanced diets, and good medical treatments.

It seemed that the situation was intensifying in this Jim Crow era, as racism was rampant and poverty was pervasive. My parents recognized early on that the best way to escape the poverty, prejudice, and poor treatment of Negroes was with a good education. Negroes were constantly in fear of being lynched for little or no reason at all. With limited opportunities and poor living conditions, our parents were determined to build our family foundation on education and moral principles. This became a never-ending theme for them.

When the day was done, Mother Dear would prepare our evening meal. Rosia was learning to be Mother Dear's helper, fetching the bowls and spoons or setting the table. Harold and I played with Delano while she cooked. Our tiny home had four bedrooms. We didn't have electricity or running water. We didn't have an inside toilet either, so we used an outhouse instead. Daddy fetched water from the well for Mother Dear to cook with. Then he fetched more water to be used for our baths after we ate. When we were finished eating, Mother Dear filled the large tin tub, bathed us, and got us ready for bed. We each got our fill of cuddling before bedtime and were probably asleep shortly after we were tucked under the covers.

In the morning, the same routines started all over. Mother Dear was up first to prepare something for breakfast and to lay out all of our clothes. Daddy was up preparing for the day, depending on the season, the crops, and which tools and animals were needed for that day's work. It was either time to plow, time to plant, or time to harvest. Harold and I were next to rise and help Daddy with whatever he needed. I was the only one in school at the time, so on school days I made sure to gather my assignments. Helping Daddy in the fields was our bonding time. Whatever needed to be done, he taught me why it had to be done a particular way and how to do it right. He explained that not following his exact ways would hurt us later down the line. Everything had an order: If you did not till the soil right, you could not plant the seeds right. If you did not plant the seeds right, the crops would not grow right. Every single step had to be done in order, every single time.

4   A Change of Plans

Daddy was an energetic sharecropper who knew that the landlord's unscrupulous practices would never allow him to progress financially. This had influenced my parents' every decision for years. The time had finally come for them to purchase land to prevent the landlord from taking any further advantage of them. Daddy decided to make the transition to own his farm and home at the appropriate time. He contacted the Federal Housing Administration (FHA) about some farm property near Alcorn Agricultural & Mechanical College in the southwestern area of Claiborne County. Although Daddy was a farmer at heart, he and Mother Dear had a long-lasting goal to live near a higher learning institution to ensure that our entire family would one day obtain college degrees.

Daddy discovered that the FHA was planning to loan money to Negro farmers, so he and Mother Dear submitted their loan application and waited to hear the results. Days passed. Then, to their surprise, they were finally approved. Daddy believed that their good fortune was due to the FHA using him and two other preachers in the community to experiment in making loans available to Negroes. All three preachers were able to purchase farm land approximating each other's. The land that Daddy purchased was 200 acres including approximately 135 acres for farming. We moved into an old home that was on the recently purchased land.

We struggled with the move to the new home because it was during a severe snow storm and ice had accumulated on the graveled roads.

In the country, there were no paved roads or highways, especially where Negroes lived. Flooded roads were prevalent with the heavy snow and rain. Our move was formidable, to say the least. The weather was not clearing, so Daddy huddled all the family into our 1937 Chevrolet to make the journey to our new home. He worried about the engine freezing since there was no antifreeze available at the time. We carried some heated water with us to douse the engine intermittently, hoping it would help keep the engine from freezing.

We had to huddle with each other since all seven of us were in the vehicle together. Mother Dear had the newest arrival at the time, Doris, in the front seat with her and Daddy. Rosia and the three boys were in the back seat. She made sure we all had blankets and quilts to keep us warm and Daddy had his gloves available in case he had to exit the car to make a repair. Mother Dear had also prepared our food for the trip and packed it conveniently for each sibling to eat while the car was moving. We did not know why they made such strategic plans for a short trip of only 25 miles. But they knew that the possibility of engine trouble and road hazards could alter the trip drastically. Daddy and his friends had previously moved most of our belongings into the home and knew that the conditions could worsen quickly.

Finally, we arrived. The new home had a kitchen, three bedrooms, and an area large enough to accommodate our old furniture and dining table. The home was poorly constructed and almost falling off the foundation. Daddy and his friends had used some type of hydraulic jack to prop up the foundation and installed some makeshift apparatus to reinforce it. The home was extremely cold, almost freezing, during the winter months. Mother Dear became an expert in insulating the areas where the air was coming into the home. She used sheets of paper from the Sears and Roebuck catalog, the Montgomery Ward catalog, and some old newspapers to plug the other areas. Mother Dear had kept the catalogs and old newspapers from year to year for the sole purpose of insulating the walls, and even the floors, in the old shack. She did not mind doing the same thing again in our new home.

The heating was a major problem as there was only one wood stove for cooking and heating the whole home. We stored our wood under the home to keep it as dry as possible. Daddy stored cords of oak and pine wood during the summer in preparation for the cold months. Even with these circumstances, our family was happy because our parents were happy. This was the first time that Daddy did not have to answer to a landlord. We saw the glow on their faces being free at last to get closer to fulfilling their dreams of home ownership and educating the family.

The next major project was to get the children of school age enrolled in school. Rosia and I were enrolled immediately at the community elementary school, Bethel. Rosia was enrolled into the first grade at age five, and I was enrolled in the second grade. I would turn seven in the middle of the school year. After a few weeks of school, Mrs. Mays, my teacher, told my parents that I was doing well.

Daddy had preached at the Mercy Seat Missionary Baptist Church for many years. My parents had developed a divine relationship with the members and chose not to seek membership in the community churches near our new home. Daddy and Mother Dear wanted to share their blessings of the new farm and home with the Mercy Seat members, as spiritual awareness and a gift from God.

At age six, it was time for me to be baptized at our church. On the night before my baptism, I was a wreck and could not sleep. I arose early Sunday morning and went through the ritual of getting ready for the baptism. Mother Dear prepared an extra set of clothes to be used after the baptism.

For the baptismal ceremony, I wore a white robe for my immersion in water. The baptism was performed by Daddy and the deacons of the congregation. Daddy also wore a white robe and he stood in the creek reciting the baptismal ceremony as I was escorted into the water. The deacon advised me to grasp my nose to avoid ingesting the water as I was immersed. I was alarmed and very apprehensive about proceeding with the baptism, but I was already too far into the water. Displaying a change of heart at this point would cause my parents, who were steadfast in their Christian principles, undue upset. I stood proudly and nervously between Daddy and the deacon. I cannot recall Daddy's exact words, but I believe he said, "I now baptize you in the name of the Father and of the Son and of the Holy Spirit" as I was immersed in the creek. I was quite relieved after it was over and proceeded to the church to change my clothes.

There was a celebration for the new inductees during the church service. After the service, food was served on the grounds for all. The food was brought to the church by members' horse-driven wagons and automobiles. We spent practically all day at church. I was drained and "churched out" to the limit. My only relief at this point would be going home. In my mind, all of the rituals were exhausting. I needed a break. Finally, after all of the well wishes from my friends and their families, we were on our way home.

Things got back to normal and I continued my assignments in school with Mrs. Mays. Soon, the school year ended and I resumed my daily chores on the farm. It was customary for me to be awakened at 5:00 a.m. on Mondays through Fridays to start my chores. It was my responsibility to feed the hogs and milk the cows before 7:00 a.m. After 7:00 a.m., my father required me to observe him bridling the horses and mules to work the farmland. It was fascinating to watch him hook the horses in tandem to generate more power to pull the heavy farm equipment. The horses and mules contributed greatly to the success of any farm year in terms of tilling, planting, harvesting the soil, and transporting farm products to the merchants.

The animals required good veterinary care to remain healthy for the arduous farm work. Daddy took pride in his beautiful horses, and even the mules, giving them the care necessary to keep them healthy. A friend of Daddy's, J.C. Dunbar, a county farm agent, was responsible for administering the medications for all the animals.

Mr. Dunbar was not a veterinarian, but he had a BS degree in agriculture and practiced animal husbandry in Claiborne County. He was a graduate of Alcorn Agricultural & Mechanical College that our family had just moved near to. Mr. Dunbar influenced me to become interested in the New Farmers of America (NFA) and the 4-H Club. I joined both organizations while in elementary school hoping to serve as an officer when I got older.

The NFA was organized around 1935 because Negroes were not allowed to join the Future Farmers of America (FFA). The FFA was for White members only. Being a member of both the NFA and 4-H afforded me the opportunity to strengthen my character, confidence, courage, academic excellence, leadership qualities, and scholarship opportunities. I participated in the county agricultural fairs by exhibiting our young calves or swine in competition for prizes. We were segregated from the main fair area, however I was so focused on winning the first-place prize that I was oblivious to our site location. Our livestock were judged by White judges in the same area that the White farmers were judged. I was in competition with Negro farmers and the judging time was set aside for only Negro contestants. Mr. Dunbar guided me and my family through all the procedures.

The 4-H Club provided a method of connecting globally with engaging youth. It instilled in me a desire to reach my fullest potential and to focus on science through agriculture. The 4-H logo was the four-leaf clover with each "H" representing the four parts of the body: head, heart, hands, and health. All 4-H

Club members were required to follow the pledge "I pledge my HEAD to clearer thinking, my HEART to greater loyalty, my HANDS to larger service, and my HEALTH to better living, for my club, my community, my country, and my world."

Each summer after the school year, Mr. Dunbar provided transportation for me to attend camp at the Piney Woods School in Mississippi. The camp was composed of both Negro youths and Mexican youths. Females from both countries also attended the camp with the males. They participated in seminars on home economics while the males concentrated on farm production. Although our co-ed seminars were conducted in the auditorium during the evening hours, the females sat on one side and the males sat on the opposite side. We co-mingled briefly for 10 to 15 minutes before the seminars ended and during that time, we could exchange ideas freely. It was an ideal system to share our cultures with each other through participation in the seminars and clinics.

The camp's main purpose was to use agriculture as a base to develop networking relationships between the two cultures. The youth had the actual experience of planting, harvesting, and preparing meals. It was a wonderful experience to participate in an actual "from-soil-to-table" delivery. During the evenings, we were advised to be in bed no later than 8:00 p.m. The dormitories for females and males were separated and heavily monitored by our camp advisors. The camp had a sort of military-style atmosphere and required adherence to the mission of the Piney Woods

School. After two to three weeks at camp, I was eager to return home with Mr. Dunbar. The camp was a mini-farm with all the demonstrations needed to produce farm products. I appreciated having the opportunity, but I could never lose sight of the racist undertones of the camp. We were completely segregated, and no Whites ever appeared on the campus during our stay there.

Upon returning home, I assumed my regular responsibilities and performed the chores that Daddy arranged for me. Even at age six, Daddy encouraged me to learn about farming by physically participating and observing him from day to day in farming techniques. I walked with him for hours as he prepared the land for planting crops. Usually, the process was to disc the soil, rake it, furrow it, plant it, and harvest it—in that order.

Daddy was extremely careful in making the distance between rows the same, regardless of the acreage for each crop (including cotton, corn, peanuts, sugar cane, soybeans, or any other legume). It was important to make sure Daddy's measurements were precise because the farm equipment was set to specific dimensions to cultivate the plants. If the dimensions of the rows were off, then the farm equipment would uproot the plants. This would cause Daddy such anguish because he had watched each of the plants sprout from their seeds. I understood why he was sensitive to this uprooting. He took quasi-ownership for the "little plants" and he set the planters carefully to protect their growth.

The harvesting usually occurred from August to September, which was a critical period of farming. Sometimes it could extend into November due to various weather conditions. The profits from our efforts were at stake because the products had to be taken to the merchants to receive our income. My parents worked very diligently, from dawn to dusk, to harvest every pound of produce to bring to market.

School opened in September and it was important to our parents that we attend the first day. This was their way to teach us to allay racism and embrace the power of an education. They knew that the County Department of Education had double standards based solely on race. White students attended school for nine months and were privileged to be bused to school. Negro students were legally allowed to stay home during the beginning of the school year to harvest the crops owned by the White landlords. This resulted in many Negro students attending school for seven or eight months out of the normal school year, preventing us from achieving a proper education. The County Department of Education was unaware that refusing to allow Negro students on the buses would not only increase our physical strength, but also develop our mental prowess and enhance our sense of community. We walked the miles to and from school chatting, teasing, and playing with each other. We supported one another and openly discussed whatever problems we were having in school. We were taught to stay together, no matter what.

There were older students who were not promoted from grade to grade in a timely manner because they started the school years late. This was due to having to harvest farm products for the White masters or landlords on the large cotton plantations. Consequently, many of the students were older when they graduated from elementary school. Most of their parents were sharecroppers or day workers. Many of the landlords were absentee owners that hired Negro managers to supervise the farm operations yearly. This included employment, transportation, payroll records, home maintenance for workers, purchasing supplies, and any other services required. The manager had total control over the people under this system and the landlord had complete confidence in this overseer. Many of these Negro families in Mississippi joined the Great Migration, relocating to Detroit, Chicago, Gary, Cleveland, and other northern cities. Gradually, the Negro population declined due to this system of mass confinement and oppression.

5   Family Farm Fun Continues

Farming was not a hobby to our parents; it was a means to a better way of life for our family. Therefore, Daddy worked all day long, six days a week, and he expected everyone in the family to have that same commitment in everything we did. He enjoyed planting every seed and watching it sprout, caring for it until it was time for the plants to be harvested. We were his "human seeds" in much the same way, and he and Mother Dear wanted to plant their family values and work ethic in each of us. Mother Dear worked the farm alongside Daddy. Each of us children took turns riding on the cotton sacks of each parent as they planted, picked, and harvested the crops, until we were old enough to carry our own sacks. When it was time to plant the next crop, again, all of us learned by example to make it a family affair.

We had a garden and an orchard in addition to the farm. Since I was not quite old enough to handle the horses and mules with the heavy farm equipment, my siblings and I were relegated to garden work. Mother Dear was a fanatical gardener who truly loved to garden. She assigned a specific gardening task to each of us. Since I was the oldest, I did the heavier work along with Mother Dear. I learned to use a hoe, pick, and shovel to establish the rows for planting.

Daddy prepared the soil, using the disc harrow to till the soil where Mother Dear's garden crops would be planted. Daddy created the furrows and sections of the plot for each crop. Mother Dear was a collector of vegetable seeds for planting. When we started the gardening process, we had several packets to choose from. There were mustard green seeds, turnip seeds, and seeds for squash, tomatoes, green peas, black-eyed peas, collards, cabbage, lettuce, watermelon, and cantaloupe.

My parents had hot beds where different seeds were planted for experimentation of growth patterns at different temperatures. After completing the rows, my siblings would bring buckets of water to saturate the soil around the new plants. I was assigned to check the plants the next day and if they were withered, I had to water them. The plants were transplanted to the regular garden after sprouting. All of the sweet potato and white potato vines were taken from the hot bed and transplanted. Daddy transplanted apple, peach, pear, fig, and pecan trees in the orchard. Our garden provided most of our daily food. Mother Dear prepared all our meals from whatever we picked. My siblings were responsible for picking the vegetables and fruit from the orchard. Rosia, Harold, and I assisted Mother Dear in preparing the food for canning. Canned foods were used during the winter months. Our meat products came from the cattle, hogs, and chickens on the farm.

Our parents encouraged all of us to pursue an education and we seldom missed a day of elementary school. I was promoted to the third grade with excellent grades, as a result of Mother Dear's dedicated tutoring and strict discipline about completing my homework daily. This year was the busiest for our family. Mother Dear had three of us in school at the same time. Rosia was in the second grade and Harold was starting first grade. Just as they had done for me and Rosia, it was Harold's turn. Mother Dear was a stickler for perfection and completeness for all of her children. It was hard when her soft love turned into tough love, but we knew it was for our own good. Daddy and Mother Dear met with all of our teachers and made sure they knew that each of us would be good students. Mother Dear continued to check all of our assignments while caring for Delano and Doris. Daddy continued to make sure we knew the importance of getting our math problems right so we would always be successful in the business.

They urged us to concentrate on our dreams and goals instead of whatever current circumstances were trying to hold us back. They knew that the schools were separate and unequal, but our family was smart enough to figure out what we needed by always working together. My parents made sure to keep our focus on what we were learning instead of being concerned about things we had no control over like the condition of the school books. They encouraged us to read as much as we could, both for pleasure and for the information we would gain. The condition of the books, whether they were hand-me-downs or had missing pages, was of little consequence. We could create our own stories from what was missing. What mattered wasn't what we didn't have, but what we had. We were poor, but we had a lot of love.

We walked to school, even in the rain and snow, but oh, how we prayed for rain. Rain meant we got a break from the farm work. Rain was truly a gift from heaven.

If it was too hot to play outside in the yard, Harold and I played in the shade underneath the front porch. We took found-wood from around the farms to build trucks. We made the wheels from the old juice and bottle tops from Mother Dear's store-bought jars. The large jar tops, attached together, became double tires for the trucks' front. Smaller jar tops were doubled, and then doubled again to make the multiple tires needed for the back of our trucks. We used old screws, nails, ropes, and wires to keep our trailers and tractors in tip top shape. We built our own roads and bridges, digging trenches in the dirt under the house. We used twigs, wood, or rocks to drive our trucks through tunnels and over bridges and rough terrain. Harold and I made a good team. Whatever we were doing, we were pretty much side-by-side. Whether we were working in the fields, playing around the house, or attending church services, we were together. That's what all families in our community were like.

I was eager to get back to school for fourth grade to engage my classmates during our play periods. My good friend Charles Rogers and I played marbles and raced against each other. He played basketball, softball, and football with me and Harold. We all also jumped rope and played hopscotch with Doris and Delano. It seemed like our group of friends who walked to and from school grew larger each year. During the winter months, we turned the treacherous weather into fun games. In the rain and sleet, we would run a few feet ahead and slide (still standing) in the mud. In the snow and ice, we had good-natured snowball fights.

We arrived at Bethel cold and wet, but we were prepared for class. Mr. Weddington, both a teacher and our principal, would arrive at school half an hour before classes started. He prided himself on having heaters to warm his students. The two classrooms for grades one through eight at Bethel were heated by kerosene or wood. We spent about half an hour getting warm and acclimated for the rigorous school day ahead.

All of the students respected Mr. Weddington, even though he was an exceedingly strict disciplinarian. If you were not following the rules, or got "out of line," you would be struck on the palms of your hands or your buttocks by a switch from one of the trees outside. This might have been child abuse at the White school. I thought Mr. Weddington was a very cruel and "evil maniac." As the principal, he was responsible for disciplining all the students. This discipline occurred throughout my elementary school experience. It left a lasting impression on me.

I entered the fifth grade under Mr. Weddington's full-time tutelage and dreaded to have to attend his classes. However, I had no other choice but to remain in the fifth grade because all parents, including mine, were dedicated to the Negro teachers in the school system. There was no such thing as a review of physical abuse by overzealous teachers, although I did believe that our teachers were devoted and faithful in encouraging and developing us academically. In our instructions, we were driven to believe that hard work and study were required to be competitive in a segregated society.

Once we reached the seventh-grade level, we could compete county-wide in reading and math. Mr. Weddington had two years to prepare us for the competition. He drilled the class in spelling, math, reading, and in singing the Negro National Anthem "Lift Every Voice and Sing." He was considered a "giant" in the Westside Community among people of all ages. Mr. Weddington was well respected and revered. His stature stood out because he walked with dignity. He was very neat and pristine, and his speech was distinct. True to his personality, he rode a White horse to school and church. He always had an unusual saddle, stirrups, spurs, and bridle for his horse, which impressed us. The saddle and accessories were lined with silver chrome to accentuate the black saddle.

Even though I despised him for his inhumane physical punishments in developing his students to achieve academic excellence, I too, admired him for his overall character. His relationship with our parents was outstanding. They believed he was invincible in supervising and teaching the students. One could not argue with his educational approach because most of his former students went on to high school and college. He was imbued with the admiration of the parents.

At the end of the school year, I was promoted to sixth grade and was glad to have a break from school. Daddy and Mother Dear made immediate plans for our summer work schedules on the farm. We knew it was difficult for our parents to clothe and feed our family. They borrowed enough money from the Port Gibson Bank to build a new home on the property after we purchased the new farm. Even then, Daddy made a promise that it would come to fruition.

Our new home construction began in 1942 and the family was elated because we had never had a newly-built home. All three homes for the Negro pastors were built around the same time in the Westside community. Our family would visit the site daily because we were exuberant about moving into a new home. We watched with anticipation as every stage of the construction was completed, from the foundation, to the walls and roof going on. Finally, it was time to move into our new home.

6 Welcome Home

The personality of our family completely changed after the move. Our parents exuded confidence and joy over this major accomplishment. They believed that the Lord had provided a path to their destiny of educating the entire family. They prayed with us children daily, thanking the Lord. Our new home was the impetus for my siblings and I to succeed in our own endeavors. We were energized to continue our studies and all of us were excited to do so in this warm home. There were no more rooms seeping with cold air; the new rooms were free of mosquitoes and flies; and the walls and floors were free of the catalog paper Mother Dear used for insulation in our old home.

Initially, we continued to use kerosene lamps for light and had no running water. The water was collected into a cistern from gutters on the roof. Rains occurred regularly and there was no shortage of water. A few years later, Daddy installed a deep well that provided running water throughout our home. Kitchen and bathroom appliances were installed to facilitate the running water. Mother Dear was overjoyed to decorate our home with very little money available. She could finally use those same Sears and Roebuck and Montgomery Ward catalogs to order the few things we needed. She ordered clothes, cooking utensils, bedroom and bathroom accessories, and other products. My siblings and I were more than excited than our parents were to have showers.

Finally, we had electricity to modernize our home. We eliminated the kerosene lamps except for our lanterns. The lanterns were used mostly for light outside. We also used them to check on the farm animals, especially in dim places where rattlesnakes sometimes were, and to caution people to stay away from a particular area. These lanterns gave off a red glow. I remember coming home with the family one evening and, to my astonishment, there was a 6-foot rattler curled up on the doorsteps leading to the family room. Daddy shot its head off with a double barrel Remington shotgun and the snake seemed to wiggle forever before dying. We were fortunate that the bullets did not ricochet and injure us.

Other poisonous snakes, including cottonmouths and copperheads, were prevalent. Most of these monsters had triangular-shaped heads and our parents taught us to use the description of the snake heads whenever we were on the lookout for them. We encountered them when prepping the fields for planting and harvesting the farm products. The rattlesnakes were numerous during the cotton-picking season and we would have to be careful because their colors blended in with the surroundings. There were small cotton houses to store the picked cotton in and different species of snakes would harbor in these houses, probably to escape the heat in a dark, quiet habitat.

Daddy and Mother Dear had worked so hard on the landlord's property with one goal in mind: to own their own land. They purchased the land close to the college with their next goal in mind. Working the farm had taken on new meaning for me. Now, it was up to all my siblings and me to follow our parents' leads. We had to combine our efforts on the farm to stay strong and help them pay the debt off. The goal was to pay the loan off as soon as possible in order to have funds to educate the entire family, including our parents, and get bachelor's degrees. Each of us children chipped in to do everything we could to help Daddy and Mother Dear, even our newest addition, Doris, now age four. She was happy to join in on all of the fun, and it was our job to make sure she was protected from the snakes and other animals.

Daddy and Mother Dear planted a garden at the new house with all of the same vegetables and fruit we had in the old garden. All of us children helped Mother Dear take care of it. We still enjoyed picking something special for her to cook for dinner. Our main farming product was cotton; however, we also produced soybeans, oats, watermelons, pecans, and corn to supplement the farm income.

As the eldest, I began taking a more active role in farming by plowing the fields, planting, and harvesting. I had watched Daddy bridle the horses and mules so many times that he finally allowed me to have my own team. I arrived in the fields at 7:00 a.m. with the horses and mules in full gear to work the land. On most occasions, my team of animals worked alongside my Daddy's team, which allowed us to have two teams working at the same time. We accomplished more or completed our farming tasks much faster, and we were able to farm larger areas for greater production. Now that I had a team, we increased our farm acreage. Dad and I would take only a short break at noon to have lunch or to water the animals. We continued to work until dusk; then the animals could relax.

My father planted legumes and grasses for the horses to graze; he wanted them healthy for hard work. The hay was derived from the grasses, legumes-alfalfa, and clover. A combination of oats and corn was also fed to the horses. We dried and baled the hay for storage to feed the cattle and horses during the severe winter months. Mr. Dunbar, the county agricultural agent, advised Daddy on the necessary feed for the animals. We planted additional acres of grasses and legumes for the cattle to graze. The cattle were also fed corn, soybean meal, cottonseed meal, and other feed. Our farm produced most of the products fed to the livestock. The sheep also grazed the field that was designated for them and were fed hay during the winter months. Year after year, the fields were replanted to provide feed for the livestock year-round.

Cotton was our main product. Picking cotton was back-breaking work because you had to stay bent over, as it grew low to the ground. The cuckle burrs—small thorny stems and twigs that grew with the cotton crops—stuck to your clothes and the cotton sacks. Cotton grew inside hard balls called cotton bolls that were about the size of a fist. The bolls would begin to open, exposing the cotton locks. After the cotton boll fully opened and dried, it formed a cotton burr that had about four or five spurs on it. It was really painful getting stuck all day long on those sharp spurs. My fingers would bleed easily, so I would lick the blood and press it against my britches for a few seconds, hoping it would stop. It wasn't a good idea to get blood all over the cotton.

The boiling sun and thick humidity added to the harsh conditions of picking cotton. It was extremely easy to get a headache from dehydration. I understood why our parents' hands were rough and calloused; my hands showed all of the same wounds from the field. My siblings and I continued picking cotton because we all had to pitch in to harvest it. Cotton was the main source of income for the family. We used cotton sacks draped over our shoulders to store the cotton as we picked. I used a very short sack in comparison to Daddy's sack and really struggled to pull it from row to row. I watched Mother Dear struggling to tow the sack strapped over her shoulder. She bent over at the waist, dragging her sack, with 60 to 70 pounds of cotton in it, down the rows, all while singing or humming the spiritual "Precious Lord Take My Hand." Daddy allowed Delano and Doris to joyride on his cotton sack as he, too, bent over at the waist, dragging more than 80 pounds and singing in harmony with Mother Dear. They sang together as if they were nearing the Promised Land. Rosia and Harold probably had small sacks to store their cotton.

Mother Dear always left the field around 11:00 a.m. to prepare our noon meal. I stayed in the fields with Daddy while she took my younger siblings with her to prepare lunch. Mother Dear put the "soul" in soul food. She cooked with "love," using the vegetables and fruits from her garden with a little meat from the farm animals. She brought the food out to us in pots and pans with forks, knives, and small towels. We used tin cups to drink from the water jugs she brought. Before the meal, we sat in a circle while Daddy offered a verse of thanks to God, then my siblings and I recited, "God's glory upon us." We truly enjoyed our meals, sheltered by the shade tree while the food stayed warm in the sun. They were a great break from the strenuous pace of work.

Mother Dear packed up the pots and pans, stored the dishes in the little storage shacks, and we all went back to picking cotton. When the day was done, she gathered everything from our lunch and we all walked back to the house.

While Mother Dear began preparations for the evening meal, Daddy and I made sure all the farm tools were put away. Rosia, Harold, and Delano played with Doris until it was time to eat. Once the meal was done, the girls helped Mother Dear clear the table and wash the dishes. Daddy read his Bible and prepared his next Sunday sermon or studied notes for meetings that he would have with the other pastors. Then it was time for showers and bed.

The cotton industry throughout Mississippi was quite successful. When our parents were sharecroppers, Daddy struggled to get a fair price from the merchants. Now that we were on our own farm, Daddy and I carried the cotton by a horse-driven wagon to Port Gibson. Each bale of cotton weighed approximately 1,300 pounds. The net weight of a cotton bale was around 500 lbs. after the seeds were extracted. The seeds were taken back to the farm to feed the farm animals. I was elated to help Daddy make the trip to Port Gibson. It was important to follow his instructions to make sure he was proud of me.

7 County Competitions & Shop Class

Summer was over, and it was time for all of us to get ready for the new school year. I entered the sixth grade happy to reunite with my schoolmates. I was especially happy to see my classmates again. I wasn't too thrilled with my teacher that year because I was being taught by Mr. Weddington. All of my classmates dreaded being in his midst. I disliked his method of punishing the students for minor offenses, myself included on occasions; I believed it was completely uncalled for or not necessary.

During the spelling bee, while writing on the blackboard, one of my classmates misspelled a word. Suddenly, Mr. Weddington tossed an eraser toward the child with great force. If a student misspelled too many words, he would pause the entire class and administer several strikes to the buttocks or the palm of the hands of the offenders with his switch. Even with bruised palms and sore buttocks, the students' parents accepted his form of discipline, including my own parents. I became petrified and frightened with the whole school atmosphere and I could no longer envision that an education was necessary. It was something I held within. I did not have the fortitude to confront my parents about this dilemma. Knowing my parents supported his actions was heartbreaking. I dared not force the issue with them and so accepted that year's school life with reservations.

There was a small glimmer of light in this gloomy situation: Mr. Weddington was very competitive. He had high standards for all Bethel students, which is probably the reason he pushed us so hard. He created an atmosphere conducive to producing cerebral and scholarly students. We were enlightened and quite literate compared to our competitors from the other schools. For this reason, I began to come around to his way of thinking. I thought perhaps the sixth grade would be the turning point of my remaining years in elementary school.

Mr. Robinson, our shop teacher, instilled confidence in me and my classmates in a different way. Mr. Robinson graduated from Alcorn Agricultural & Mechanical College with a Bachelor of Science (BS) degree in Mechanical Industries. He was a very joyful person with lots of energy and he encouraged us to excel in class with positive reinforcement. His class provided the opportunity to learn a wide array of new skills. He taught us how to repair farm implements, make light furniture—like cedar chests—and to sharpen equipment. He also taught us how to design and make oak handles for axes, hammers, shovels, and hoes.

Mr. Robinson also organized a basketball team to compete with other elementary and high schools. Both female and male basketball teams performed well under Mr. Robinson and this was an exhilarating period for the students. We were so energized in helping to construct the basketball goals and we marked the court boundaries without any coercion. None of us had to be persuaded to participate in completing the project and it was a piece of cake with our excitement and cheerfulness. We had a solid-surface, earth diamond to play on, and spent hours clearing weeds with hoes, shovels, and other shop tools. The older school boys from the community could play on the male team because we competed against some high schools.

We had really begun to like school because being on the basketball teams was a social outlet from the rigid and strict academic scene created by Mr. Weddington. There were no rules governing basketball play for Negro schools. Elementary schools frequently played against high schools. Some of the coaches recruited players, if they did not look too out of place, to be on either the elementary or high school team. The students were so pumped up on game day, they could not concentrate on their studies. All of the players looked forward to the new uniforms and knee pads. This was "big time basketball" for us and it was something totally new for our small poverty-stricken community.

The White elementary schools had attractive blacktop or concrete courts for basketball with clear markings and nets on the rims. As a Negro student, I wondered how exciting it would be playing on their courts. Our backboards and hoops at Bethel were poorly constructed with markings that were barely legible. Again, we were powerless to correct such injustices, so we concentrated on enjoying playing our game, knowing that we had the best team.

Daddy and Mother Dear encouraged my siblings and I to reach for excellence in the pursuit of an education, repeating and drilling into us, "Education...Education...Education!" An education, for many of the students, was the only way out of their circumstances.

Most of the students were poor and not well-fed. They did not have balanced diets and often came to school hungry. The government provided food rations to be shared among many of my schoolmates. Canned pork and beans, pounds of cheese, and powdered milk were consumed by the Negro students in this program. The rations were controlled by the Claiborne County Department of Education. Naturally, according to our Negro teachers, the White students received the nutritious rations. The Negro students had very little powdered milk, regular milk, vegetables, or juices in their diet. Rickets was a frequent childhood disease among us, resulting from a vitamin D deficiency. Our communities suffered from many childhood diseases from the inefficient conditions in the school facilities, which were never addressed or improved. I think my siblings and I were too poor to be sick. We probably worked the germs right out of us on the farm.

Bethel was very cold during the winter and very, very hot during the summer. During the summer, the heat was stifling and the humidity was high. The windows were left open in hope for a breeze. We were inundated with mosquitoes and flies.

My brothers and I encountered some "little thugs" in our school that were hellbent on fighting every day as we walked home from school. I dreaded these attacks. We often waited around for Mr. Weddington to depart with us, for some protection. Finally, I told him about these rascals and they were scolded for their acts. Our father lectured us to defend ourselves, but we chose not to fight outright, and the bullies took full advantage of that. They did not end the attacks until one day my brother, Harold, leveled one of them into a state of unconsciousness. That was the end of anyone bothering us, and we were never stressed about walking home from school again.

During the school season, we were not bused to and from school as the White kids were. The Price family was a White family who lived two homes below us on the same graveled road. They had three boys and we often played sports with them—football, softball, baseball, and track. They were very friendly, and we visited each other's homes. Mr. Price was the bus driver for the White kids, who drove by the Negro students walking to school in the morning. On rainy or snowy days, the bus would splash water and dirt on the Negro students because there were no sidewalks. The White students laughed and made faces at us from the bus windows. The road we lived on was also very dusty. During the summer months, the bus rode by the Negro students, raising a big ball of dust and gravel into the air. We inhaled this sediment and the White students laughed so hard they were bent over in their seats. This did not discourage us from playing sports with the Price boys, though, and they looked forward to playing with us. This was an unusual pairing, but sports had a way of crossing all racial lines.

The school year ended on a high note because our parents were satisfied with our grades. Rosia had done very well in fifth grade, Harold had finished fourth grade, and Delano had happily been promoted to third grade. The principal advised our parents that I could skip seventh grade and be promoted to eighth grade. Daddy and Mother Dear discussed the matter in private, and then consulted with me. They concluded that I should remain in the seventh grade because the students in the eighth grade were older and, in some cases, much older. The eighth grade included older students repeating it and older students returning to it after being absent for a year or more. It was not an environment my parents wanted for me, so it was decided unanimously that I would remain among my peers.

By now, I was aware of the approaching season for farming and planning. Daddy and the other two preachers purchased a farm tractor together to aid in increasing farm production. Horse teams were gradually becoming obsolete because farmers were reducing manual labor and producing more with tractors. Daddy and the two preachers alternated days using the tractor. The preachers were the first Negroes to own a tractor in the community.

The other preachers and their families were like family to us. We kept each other's children as needed and the parents spoke to each other's children if they did something inappropriate. The parents provided shelter, food, or anything else essential in lean times and we all shared our food. It was like a colossal village.

Our profits were twofold for that year and our family revered the additional farm equipment. I was happier than Daddy because it meant I spent less time plowing the field with horses in the extreme heat and humidity. I cannot explain how laborious it was under those conditions, perspiration always dripping from my face and body. We drank water constantly to avoid dehydration. Using the tractors was a welcome relief in many ways.

Each summer, we went through the same ritual of suffering from the heat during the days of picking cotton. As we got older, each family member had to drag their own cotton sack with a strap over their shoulders. Imagine dragging a sack of cotton weighing approximately 50 to 70 pounds from row to row in the heat daily, bent over at the waist so as not to miss anything. This was quite inhumane, but we all understood what the mission of the family was. By the end of the day, Mother Dear hummed, "Brighter days will come" and she was accurate.

We replanted the same crops from year to year and our work ethics never waned. The tractor allowed us to have higher yields, which meant we had more acreage for crops and quicker harvests. The summer months were quite long, and I was beginning to tire of the field work and the work around home. Daddy always had a job for me, including mowing the lawn, cutting locust posts for fencing, clearing ditches for water drainage, and terracing to avoid soil erosion and retention of nutrients. There was time allotted for picking fruit and assisting Mother Dear in canning for the winter months. Most of these chores were performed when the fields were too wet from rain for any farm activity.

Finally, at age 11, I entered the seventh grade and took a break from the arduous farm work. I did not have the courage to complain to my parents about the work and I wanted to demonstrate my fortitude. My school experience became enriching because the principal had begun to allow students to go to the blackboards to explain their homework. Spelling and math were my favorite subjects, though I also excelled in history.

Mother Dear monitored my writing assignments and wanted every letter to be perfect. If each letter was not distinct, I had to do it over and over. For every math assignment, Daddy reviewed each problem with me. He emphasized not just memorization, but also analysis of a thought or idea.

I was still passionate about the workshop in Mr. Robinson's class. I was good at repairing farm tools, constructing cedar chests for magazines, making axe handles from different types of wood, and building small model homes. Mr. Robinson's basketball acumen continued to be popular throughout the school year and we were more than excited to play.

Mr. Weddington was persistent in his belief that knowledge was the foundation of being a good citizen, and it provided an environment in which each student could attain the highest level of their life's ambition. He enjoyed having all the students sing and memorize The Negro National Anthem "Lift Every Voice and Sing" (composed by James Weldon Johnson). He required us to sing it over and over and I believed he was inspired by the words. I remember that his favorite lines were "We have come over a way that with tears has been watered; we have come, treading our path through the blood of the slaughtered." I knew they were his favorite because his facial expression changed at that part of the second verse. The anthem bonded us. It also inspired us to succeed, despite the limitations of our current circumstances, with faith and hope that "We will forever stand, true to our God, true to our native land."

8 Taking on More Responsibility

During the school year, my father encouraged me to sell newspapers on Saturdays in Port Gibson. He wanted me to have an independent job that allowed me to experience the "handling of my own money and business." Negroes were not permitted to sell White newspapers. We consulted the editor, Edgar T. Crisler, about selling the Port Gibson *Reveille* — the White paper — to no avail. The *Reveille* was one of the oldest newspapers in Mississippi and was an independently owned paper. I do not recall the *Reveille* publishing anything positive about Negroes when I was young. The only thing mainstream White newspapers published about Negroes were news events that were derogatory and degrading.

My father and I did some research on Negro newspapers. We decided to sell two weekly newspapers, primarily to provide Mississippi Negro news and national Negro news. *The Delta Leader*, published in Greenville, Mississippi, was chosen for Mississippi news and the *Pittsburgh Courier* was selected for national news. I received 50 copies of each newspaper weekly and sold them every Saturday to Negroes in Port Gibson. It was not difficult to sell the papers because it was the only way for Negroes to receive national news. Most of the time I sold the papers for 25 cents, however if a person did not have enough money, I accepted whatever they could afford.

After I finished selling my newspapers, I visited my favorite ice cream parlor, Seale Lily. Seale Lily had a single entrance for Negroes and

Whites. However, after entering, Negroes went to the left and Whites to the right to place an order, separated by a rope extending to the counter. For five cents you could buy the smallest ice cream cone in any flavor. The Negro female employees could serve Negroes and Whites but were not granted permission to operate the cash register. Only a White person tended the cash register, usually a female.

Negroes had to leave the facility immediately to eat their ice cream or milkshake out on the streets. On very hot and humid days, the ice cream cone would drip on your fingers and hand almost immediately. Because of this, I ate my cones with speed. The Whites could remain in the parlor to eat and relax in an "airy" setting.

Department stores were owned by Jews but employed Negro females. Negro customers were also not allowed to try on clothes or shoes in the store, but could take their belongings home and return them if they didn't fit or weren't wanted. This practice was used because Whites wouldn't patronize the stores if they knew or witnessed that Negroes operated the cash register and tried on apparel and shoes. This was quite amusing to the Negroes who watched as the Jewish owners placed the returned apparel or shoes right back on the shelf for sale to the general public. The owners were sympathetic to Negroes in a covert manner but dared not contradict the Jim Crow system publicly. Many Jews donated anonymously for the advancement of Negroes by employment and cash donations. I even believed that the Jewish store owners would have allowed

Negro females to operate the cash register if it were not for the Jim Crow system.

White people in Claiborne County and Mississippi exhibited hatred and directed indescribably racist tactics toward Negroes. As a boy, I witnessed young Negro men beaten until bloody, unable to protect themselves or receive protection from the White police. White men especially seemed to relish police brutality. Young Negro men were jailed and beaten by the police while in custody. As a young teenager, I often feared being harassed by White police officers. I was careful to cross over to the other side of the street if they came in my direction. My parents had prepared me to be cautious and not resist their aggressiveness if I was ever confronted or detained by them. There was little chance of survival.

During the beatings, there were usually several officers involved. It was almost like a lynching and the Negroes observing it, who outnumbered the Whites, left as quickly as possible, without drawing attention to themselves. These scenes engendered anxiety, fear, and distrust of the White men. White women elicited much more courtesy toward Negroes. This was probably because Negro females logged long hours in their homes cleaning, ironing, doing laundry, cooking, serving meals, caring for their children, running errands, and doing all the chores one would expect the married White lady to do for herself. Negro women walked a thin line. They had to explain to others that their actions were tied to filling an urgent request by the White lady of the house, praying to assuage anger.

I completed the seventh grade as an honor student. At the end of the year, I had surpassed my parents' expectations and was praised to remain steadfast. I continued my yearly enrichment camp at the Piney Woods School with Mr. Dunbar. Over the years, the school had expanded in size and programs. The camp provided seminars and lectures in Math, Science, English, and Agriculture. Piney Woods was considered a top boarding prep school in Mississippi with a year-round curriculum for Negroes. International students also attended the school.

I returned home to assist Daddy with the farm work, determined to aid in increasing production. I was energized by the information I received from the enrichment camp. It was my desire to use the theory of agricultural production I gained from the camp to expand our production. Daddy purchased a second, small ford tractor to boost our capability of producing more. This tractor was used in conjunction with the larger tractor to prepare more fields for farming.

Daddy leased more land in the community to plant crops for higher yields, including the base products of cotton and corn. Surprisingly, the largest land lease was from a White owner, although other leases were with Negro owners. The land leased from the White owner was quite fertile and produced abundant vegetation and crops. Daddy knew a lot about soil and determined that the very dark-colored soil was rich for farming. The Piney Woods' seminars confirmed the same. The land was located near a river bottom and did, indeed, have good soil.

Now, at age 12, Daddy taught me how to operate the Ford tractor. We drove the tractors in tandem when preparing the soil for the crops. Daddy always drove the large tractor and took the lead.

The horse-driven equipment had become obsolete and the horses were now mostly for pleasure riding. Our cattle herd, hogs, and sheep had increased considerably. We stopped slaughtering the livestock ourselves and carried our livestock to the slaughterhouse to be cut and packaged for us. Mother Dear continued her gardening and canning in a timely manner and the family subsisted mostly on homegrown food year-round. Rosia and Doris were happy to help Mother Dear because they were often the first to taste whatever they were canning. Our farm production reached a high plateau with the leasing of additional land and the utilization of farm machinery. The cotton production skyrocketed to new levels, increasing our trips to the gin in Port Gibson.

Daddy hired a few field hands who helped me assemble the cotton into the trailers for transportation. It was our responsibility to load the cotton on the trailers the evening before. This allowed us to leave at daybreak, around 5:00 a.m., to transport the cotton. It was a winding trip on a rough, dusty, gravel road with numerous potholes. The road was narrow and often we had to pull over and allow oncoming traffic to pass. With the horrific, dusty conditions from the traffic, it required much skill for us to maneuver the tractors, each pulling two trailers of cotton.

At the gin, I went first because Daddy had instructed me on how to avoid being cheated by the White gin operator. I knew the total weight of the cotton. When the seeds were separated from the cotton, it was easy to add the cotton weight plus seed weight to equal the total bale weight. After my first visit, I never had another problem with the gin operator. The round trip encompassed about 30 miles. We arrived back home in the early afternoon, then the same rotation of farm work began again.

By this period, Daddy was hiring more field hands to assist in producing higher yields. Our family had a genuine relationship with them because we stood side by side, chopping and picking cotton, or working on whatever project was being done. We treated them like family; some were members of Daddy's congregation. We supplied them with water and food. I had the additional responsibility of providing transportation for them to and from the farm. They worked during the summer beginning in May and ending late in September.

The end of every summer was tiring. The summer preceding my eighth-grade school year was no exception. The older I got, the longer the days seemed to last. I was physically exhausted from work, work, and more work, but happy for Daddy that the business was doing so well. I pleaded for the school year to commence, wondering if there was better work than farming to do, or whether I wanted to continue farming indefinitely. School started and after a week, I was a happy camper. During the first few weeks, even though I was in school, I occasionally provided transportation for the field hands in the early morning and late afternoon.

In school, preparation was underway for the county-wide competition. The students concentrated on reading, history, and math. It was an honor for a school to be declared the Negro County Education Champion. It was intense for the students chosen by the teaching staff to represent Bethel. Our classmates became engrossed in all subject matters, concentrating on winning the prize. It was amusing hearing our teachers' ideas for preparing us for this fierce competition. Later in the school year, Mr. Weddington chose the "combatants" to quest for this coveted achievement.

I was selected as one of the participants for reading comprehension and speed reading. We reviewed our subject matter by rotating between teachers for a broader preparation. The teachers would huddle and then advise us on our weak points. Mr. Weddington made the final decision on our training and the techniques we would use in competition. It was extensive and exhaustive, not only the reading and math portion, but also standing in front of the class and spelling out words, even going to the blackboard to write them. Nevertheless, these procedures prompted us to perform with stellar self-confidence at the county competitions. We were absolutely prepared when the contests began. I took first prize for reading and comprehension. My parents, teachers, and classmates were elated with my performance. For winning, I was presented with a mini-bible. All of us were excited as my classmates excelled in their presentations. Bethel was awarded first place; we were the Negro County Education Champion.

Throughout the school year, shop class and sports continued to be an outlet for me to both excel and relax in. As my skills increased, so did my determination and tenacity. The collaboration and synergy I gained with my teammates originated with the work ethic my parents planted within me. The team continued to compete with the elementary and high schools in the area. Our Christmas play, the crowning event of each school year, was another integral part of my academic excellence. The Parent Teacher Association members made the costumes for every Christmas theme. Rehearsals and acting were as unsettling for me at this age as the Easter play was when I was younger. At least back then it was preceded by an Easter egg hunt and a treat of my favorite chocolate-covered eggs.

True to my parents' vision, I was exposed to so many opportunities. I understood the gravity of their goals. They were correct that all the knowledge and skills I garnered to this point belonged to me, never to be taken away. I graduated from elementary school in the spring of 1945.

9   Closer to the End Goal

Mississippi racism had taken on a different meaning for me. Stories from my parents and grandmother were impactful; I felt for them and what they had to go through. However, the common lynchings and beatings of Negroes had become part of my own experience. Our Westside community in Claiborne County was isolated, to some extent, from the actual killings and beatings in other areas of Claiborne County and Mississippi, but I watched my steps; I watched my surroundings; and I was always aware of who was watching me. It was uncomfortable and unnerving. I knew, also, that the proximity of our home to Alcorn Agricultural & Mechanical College helped keep our small community from being infiltrated by the Ku Klux Klan (KKK) and other hate groups. Even so, that feeling of always having to look over my shoulder was becoming more ingrained.

The location of our community was unique because there were only two major exits off the main highway. One went straight through to the college and the other went west, connecting on to Port Gibson. Perhaps the entrance and exit were constructed by God to protect us from the KKK's overt attacks.

Every family in our community constantly drummed into us the seriousness of avoiding these racial conflicts for our own protection. The families in our community also let it be known that they would avenge any malicious invasion in our small community.

As the oldest of the siblings, what weighed heavy on my mind were my brothers and sisters. Each of my siblings added an extra measure of responsibility for me to lead by example. All during my elementary school years, our parents used the farm to teach us the importance of working together. As Daddy preached at the four churches, we learned that being blessed and blessing others only compounded our own blessings. From every teacher, Mrs. Shaffer, Mr. Dunbar, Mr. Weddington, and Mr. Robinson, I learned what the strong bonds of community and teamwork actually meant.

Life in the small towns and unincorporated areas in Mississippi scarcely hid the remains of Negroes taken from the jails and murdered by mobs of White men, their bodies disposed of in rivers or elsewhere. There was no justice. Now, entering high school, I began to be fearful of White people and despised them for their cowardly acts against Negroes. I tried not to exhibit hate toward them because Daddy taught me not to exemplify abhorrence toward mankind, but it was so difficult to love them. During this period, I discovered that my parents were truly righteous in their vision for our family.

The farm was waiting for me to return full-time. Our farm plans indicated that the increase production was dependent upon expanding the land leases for additional crops to be planted. It also brought about a greater role and responsibility for me to undertake as the operator of the second tractor. More land leases were acquired, and the game was on for increasing production. Daddy and I drove the tractors from 7:00 a.m. to 8:00 p.m. daily in preparation for planting. It was pretty ambitious for the first few weeks in operating the machinery, however the heat and humidity had begun to snuff out my enthusiasm and energy. Again, I was reluctant to let Daddy know my true feelings, for fear of ruining his plans for the family to have a productive year. I sincerely did not want to disappoint him in any way.

We had decided that I would skip the camp at Piney Woods School and concentrate on farming. Our work was indeed rewarding for the year. In 1945, we had bumper products in cotton, corn, and the other crops. The field hands remained committed to our family and assisted us with everything from planting to harvesting. They were very loyal and proved their ability to work independently. Our family still had great relationships with them and invited them to dine with us on many occasions.

We were blessed to have such a successful farm year. Daddy reported that our proceeds were exceptional, and he was able to give bonuses to some of the managers of the different crops. This was on top of the substantial payment he made on the FHA loan, allowing him to reduce the balance enough to better manage it going forward. It was a jubilant and joyous time for our family with this achievement. Mother Dear would always remind us of one of her favorite premonitions: "Brighter days for the future." For me, it brought focus to our leaner times when it wasn't so easy to purchase clothes or shoes for us.

Mother Dear spent many nights fashioning clothes from scraps of cloth. She had a keen eye for what suited each of us. She made our quilts, too. Likewise, Daddy was innovative in restoring our shoes. He used hog rings to re-attach soles to our shoes; patterned paste board and a rubber-like material to put in our shoes when a hole appeared in the soles; and twine instead of shoe strings. Together, my parents made sure that hand-me-down clothes were passed from one child to another with love and care. Mother Dear also had great culinary skills, possessing an uncanny ability to provide complete, tasty meals for us from very little food. Intuitively, she planned for the nourishment of our family using the vegetables and fruits she planted in her gardens.

She and Daddy worked their fingers tirelessly to make sure they realized their dreams for our family. They set goals, determined to provide us with a better life. After a resounding year of farming, our family purchased a new 1945 Chevrolet for approximately $900. Dependable transportation was important for our large family, as Daddy was the pastor for three congregations now.

Daddy and Mother Dear already determined that I would not attend Port Gibson High School because very few of their students went on to college. They wanted me to attend Alcorn Agricultural & Mechanical College Prep High School, believing that the college environment would induce their children to pursue college degrees. I had other plans. A few days before registration for high school, I informed my parents that I was not interested in attending. Internally, I wanted to follow the path of my close elementary school classmates in the great Negro migration to the North. I had become disillusioned with the hard farm work as well as the climate in Mississippi. I thought that surely there must be something better someplace else.

My parents peered at me with utter shock and awe, dismayed beyond belief. Daddy was speechless only for a moment, chiding, "Eugene, you are out of your mind. You are only 13 years old. How will you survive with an elementary school education as a Negro?" He was visibly perplexed and said, "I have a solution. Tomorrow morning, you will be awakened at 4:30 a.m. and the two of us will drive our tractors from 6:00 a.m. 'til around 8:00 p.m., only taking a break for a meal."

We plowed the land for two days with the same zeal. By the end of the second day, I begged my father to stop and promised him that I would enroll in school if given another chance. He responded, "Eugene, are you absolutely sure? Because if you are not going to high school, this will be your daily job." I said, "Yes," and he nodded gleefully, "You may enroll." The following day I registered in the college prep high school.

Being on a college campus as a high school student was intriguing at first. Since the preparatory high school was on the college campus, all the high school students had access to the college library, labs, dining hall, medical dispensary, and any other facilities. Some students were veterans. Other high school students were living in the dormitories with the college students. The day students included college faculty members' children and a few students from the community. The high school was academically challenging, requiring conscientious effort from the students. The faculty included college professors as well as regular high school teachers. Most of the high school teachers had advanced degrees and some were married to college professors.

At age 13, during my first year of high school, I joined the day-student population. Daddy knew the right White person to assist him in obtaining a temporary driver's permit, so I was able to drive myself to school many times. I was very diligent about getting home immediately after classes ended. When I drove our vehicle, a stack of bricks in the seat allowed me to best see the roadway. Without the bricks, I was not tall enough to see clearly over the dashboard.

At home, before doing my schoolwork, I assisted with family tasks for a few hours. All of us children chipped in to finish family projects. Each evening, my parents demanded I complete the teacher's lesson plan before retiring for the night. After ending elementary school with honors, I did not fully engage myself in my high school work. Now, in my teenage years, I thought I knew as much about life as my parents. My rebellious behavior was attributed to my excitement about college sports and the social environment. The high school had a basketball team that was coached by college Physical Education students. It was *electrifying* to compete for a chance to play an organized sport, even though I did not have the time to practice or play because of our farm work schedule.

Thankfully, I finished my first high school year as a B student. The following summer was refreshing. I returned to the Piney Woods School camp, now with the high schoolers. There, we did experiments on raising and lowering temperatures of hot beds to determine the growth patterns of plants before they were transplanted. Cattle manure was used in increments to control the temperature as desired and the school's livestock played a role in the compost used for the experiments.

Our evening social interactions with the schoolgirls were overseen by male and female chaperones. The camp population was diverse and included students from South America. Piney Woods built character and reinforced a community of pride for all students, particularly for Negroes.

Returning to the farm for the summer was business as usual. Daddy purchased new, more advanced farm equipment from the International Harvester Company, including a Model H Farmall tractor, used for general or light farm work. The John Deere tractor, a workhorse, was added for heavy farm work such as constructing farm ponds, terracing difficult landscapes, and logging. Daddy made it clear that the John Deere tractor was off limits for me until my senior year of high school.

Our family achieved another banner year of farming as the cotton crop reached new heights. Our field hands and managers remained indispensable in their performances and were truly extended family by now. Soon, it was time for me to return to school and I was ready to leave the domain of strenuous farming.

Daddy's reputation broadened. He was elected Moderator of the Claiborne County Negro Missionary Baptist Association. This was considered a prestigious position in the community and respect for him grew immensely, even among Whites. The Port Gibson Bank, owned and operated by Mr. Robert Gage, provided loans to our family as needed because of Daddy's good payment history. Both Negroes and Whites recognized this. Daddy understood more than I how his accomplishments were perceived. His decisions were calculated and measured; he balanced on that invisible line between helping his family get ahead and keeping his family safe. Mr. Gage illustrated that there were caring people in every race. There was a group of quiet White people who aided or attempted to advance relationships with Negroes, even in Mississippi.

At this point, I was helping my parents by driving my siblings to school. I dropped Harold, Delano, and Doris off at the Alcorn Elementary Prep School, and then took Rosia with me to the Alcorn Prep High School for her freshman year. My sophomore classmates and I were motivated to excel in our classwork. Mrs. Jackson, the assistant principal, had by now established a spirit of academic excellence in her students. However, her great teaching methods eluded me. She exhibited a brilliance incomparable to any of my former teachers, but I just could not take full advantage of her talents. Once again, I did not apply my God-given academic abilities. I was satisfied with passing grades.

My interest was in shop and the mechanical industries. In shop class, we learned to use the T-square and other instruments for the construction of mechanical drawings. The high school students constructed large cedar chests, light furniture, and small model buildings.

My classmates were a closely-knit group that shared ideas, notes, and engaged with each other. We shared snacks and assisted each other with classwork. Because the population exceeded 100 students, the teachers developed all their classes into successfully interconnected units. Their dedication and loyalty moved from student to student throughout the school.

Mrs. Jackson knew how blessed we were to have this opportunity for a superior education among the many Negro injustices caused by Whites. She would not accept any excuses for poor performance, knowing we had no idea what she knew. Most of the Negro high schools in the Claiborne County community and the greater state of Mississippi were inferior, degraded facilities. They had poorly-trained teachers and lacked all of the necessary tools for academic excellence including supplies, books, and libraries. They had underfunded or non-existent science labs as well as equally-inferior or non-existent curricula, sports facilities, transportation, accountability for truancy, organized PTA, and counseling services. The KKK and other White hate groups promoted killings and night-rides to instill fear, even toward other Whites who were sympathetic to Negroes.

As Negro high school students, considering the oppression and suffering caused by the Jim

Crow laws, it felt like we were chosen in the eyes of God, both in Claiborne County and the greater state of Mississippi. Negroes were completely isolated from mainstream society in every aspect including opportunities, education, and health-care. Jim Crow Mississippi was comparable to apartheid in South Africa. My parents invariably repeated their advice for me to excel in school. Daddy often said, "Whites may kill you, but they are unable to destroy your knowledge while living."

That year, our farm was as productive as the previous year in every aspect. My major job was transporting cotton to the gin. The farm had become more automated in harvesting, and larger loads of cotton were carried to the gin to be separated from the seeds. Profits increased; my parents were elated and blessed. I experienced less pressure as the oldest sibling to lead by example. Each of my brothers and sisters were gifted with the same parental guidance I had. Daddy and Mother Dear recognized each of their kids' strong points and the things they enjoyed.

10 Campus Life and Civil Rights

By the end of the summer, as usual, I craved to escape from farm work. Laboring in the same awful heat and humidity had only intensified. Finally, my junior year of high school arrived. The teachers outlined their expectations, visions, and goals for the year, making it clear that more discipline on my part was required. I had to come to terms with my own lack of self-discipline and what it would ultimately cost me. I wrestled with my own conformity and lost. I chose to continue to produce less in a time where the opportunities I had required more, though I did not deliberately rebel against classwork.

My teacher sent messages to my parents regarding my attitude. Daddy and Mother Dear did not question her motives or findings. They scheduled an appointment with Mrs. Jackson. My parents knew that I did not want to confront Mrs. Jackson because she commanded respect and dignity, so they deliberately set the appointment with her instead of the principal, Mr. Wilson. Mrs. Jackson was straightforward and stated her position clearly to my parents. She shared her frustration that I was choosing not to reach my potential by doing just enough to be average. My parents cringed at the word "average" as if it had been seared right through their hearts. They let her words sit in silence.

Mrs. Jackson's message, unfortunately, did not translate into better academic excellence for me. My know-it-all attitude invaded my inner character, dispelling any academic goals in its path. I could neither explain why I chose not to fully engage academically, nor explain the full extent of my dissent. I completed my third year of high school with better than average grades, but nothing was pleasurable.

I knew how I spent my summer was already determined—I was expected to become part of the farm workforce again. I knew Daddy and Mother Dear were unhappy with my scholastic performance, but once again, they had to teach me a much more valuable lesson. They were silent yet watchful of my activities, keeping me focused and busy enough to stay within that invisible line. They prayed I would find my way through my mental turmoil. Thankfully, we reached our profit and income goals that year. The time was approaching to get back to school for my senior year. I could not wait to be relieved from all the hectic chores.

The school year began with more ease than previous ones. I had even begun to think about going to college. I was 16 years old and confident in my decision-making abilities. Daddy and Mother Dear had always been open and willing to listen and discuss anything with their children, even if they eventually refused our requests. I was thankful to them for that, knowing that my recent actions had not met their expectations. I presented my case, answered their questions, and waited for them to deliberate. I was blessed that they agreed to collaborate with me in finalizing the decisions for my education.

Daddy acquired a new 1949 Chevrolet sedan for safe, reliable transportation to and from the campus. By now, all my siblings were used to me driving them to school when I could. Some days, we had to walk together to and from school.

After returning home from school, my brothers and I filled in the gaps when farm work was needed while my sisters helped Mother Dear prepare the evening meal. All our homework assignments were completed before bedtime. Churchgoing was still mandatory. We spent all day, each Sunday, in church. Driving the new car neutralized some of my boredom in church. Daddy was now pastor for four churches. This meant I had to attend each church on Sundays. Daddy was confident with me driving him to his churches, which became a routine Sunday task, even if, on occasion, no one except the two of us attended the services.

On one such occasion, we were returning from Mt. Olive Missionary Baptist Church in Red Lick, Mississippi on a beautiful Sunday afternoon. Daddy always drove when passing through Fayette, Mississippi, which was a hot bed for White racists. That day, we stopped in Fayette and parked near the ice company to purchase some ice to bring home. As we returned to the car, a White police officer, in his early 20s, approached Daddy and inquired about how he had parked, accusing him of not parking close enough to the curb. Underneath, he really wanted to know about the new car and where it was purchased.

Fayette was mostly a Negro town, but that didn't stop Negroes from being harassed by Whites. The police officer addressed Daddy as "Uncle" and asked where he got that car from. (It was common for younger White males to refer to older Negro men as "Uncle.") Daddy mused and chose not to respond to the officer. When the young man became inflamed, Daddy saw his hostility and said that he was a country preacher returning from church service, which diffused the situation. We quickly exited the town. I realized I had witnessed Daddy's resolve in a racist confrontation. I remained quiet for the rest of the ride home. This could have been very different if the whole family was with us. Perhaps Daddy would not have stopped that day.

Life went on as normal. On other Sundays, our family still followed the customary agenda of visiting relatives and arriving home early in the evenings. We remained dutiful in our actions and demeanor in each location. Daddy was always overly protective on the road, careful not to endanger the family. I had spent most of my life watching, learning, and following his guidance. I sensed the gravity of his responsibility to avoid any danger. However, I was also growing weary of attending church. I was "churched out." I desired a change and even thought of asking my parents if I could attend vesper services on Alcorn's campus instead of attending regular church services. I broached the subject, but my parents had deaf ears.

Hoping to get relief in other ways, I tried to get permission to drive the car on Saturdays for away-games of football and basketball, to no avail. Mother Dear, ever the strong disciplinarian, did not trust me to drive to such events. I pleaded my case to go to a nightclub with my friends. Again, Mother Dear made sure I understood that she had no intention of letting me go to "those" places. Thinking I could appeal to her gentler side, I asked her if she thought I was better than my friends. Mother Dear stopped what she was doing and stood up close to me. She looked directly into my eyes and responded, "You *are* better because you are not going to hang out with 'those' people who are doing 'those' things." I did not pursue the issue any further. Mother Dear was unwavering in her control of our social interactions. I dared not show my frustrations about what she considered "typical teenage concerns" (i.e., work-life, church-life, and the lack of a social life).

Senior year was off to a bang with the influx of new students and more veterans from World War II. I settled into my classes. Being on the same campus with the college students provided me with a broader narrative for my future. Medgar Evers, a 24-year-old WWII veteran, was beginning his education at Alcorn Agricultural & Mechanical College at the same time that I began my senior year at Alcorn Prep High School. In his first year, Medgar quickly became a central figure on campus. He competed on the debate, football, and track teams. I began to cross paths with Medgar and his older brother Charles. (Charles, who was also a WWII veteran returning to college, was in his sophomore year at Alcorn.) Medgar emitted class and dignity; love and caring; and portrayed a sincere concern for everyone around him. From my vantage point, he carried himself with the decorum of a minister—a "divine prophet" leading his flock to freedom. We high school students were his flock. He lectured us to excel and reach for the highest ideals in education.

Medgar challenged us in social gatherings to be respectful; to study diligently; to treat one as you would like to be treated; and to know that nothing is impossible. He encouraged us to remain in school and focus on creating justice for all people. Both Medgar and Charles seemed to be sincere about bringing the injustices toward Negroes to an end. Charles was more physically confrontational and less obliging to Whites than Medgar was.

During this school year, some of the high school students enrolled in a college music appreciation course supervised by the college chair of the music department. The course was in the Oakland Memorial Chapel on campus. Medgar came to our class while we were singing and joined in. We sang "Lift Every Voice and Sing." Medgar had a beautiful voice and remained close with us from that day forward. He continued to focus on the racial injustices in Mississippi. His vision was to eliminate all the suffering, reverse the Jim Crow laws, and dismantle the KKK by boycotting White businesses. Many of the college students did not think this was feasible and feared being expelled if they participated. Several veterans and other students were sympathetic to his ideas and joined in unauthorized group meetings on the campus lawn. The administration witnessed the student gatherings with consternation; they feared that the Governor's office or other authorities would reprimand the college by closing it.

Practically all the students who entered high school with me in 1945 were set to graduate with me. Our class was united in our goal of achieving academic victory. None of us wanted the campus to be shut down. Principal Wilson inspired us to challenge the "status quo" and exceed his expectations for educational excellence. He guided the younger students, influenced by the veterans, to not take the wrong path while pursuing their educational aspirations.

Assistant Principal Jackson insisted we take full advantage of the college library's periodicals to cover a wide range of subjects. We completed assignments in English literature, grammar, and history, all of which required us to spend a lot of time in the library. Mrs. Jackson wanted to instill her love of reading and writing in all of us. Our other teachers in math and chemistry imparted the same wisdom and gave us any assistance we needed including counseling, tutoring, and encouragement.

I graduated from high school in 1949. The usual farm routines continued throughout the summer.

11 First to Enter College

Daddy and Mother Dear had dreamed of the day I entered college before I was even born. They had tilled and toiled in the sweltering Mississippi heat and humidity as sharecroppers, hoping to fulfill a lifetime legacy of education for their family. They had spent every waking moment as an indestructible united force, driven to achieve the goal of a college education, engaging with every teacher, reviewing every assignment, and attending every school session. Mother Dear trusted and respected every dream that Daddy had of providing a better life for her and the family.

I was ecstatic and overwhelmed as the first from my family to attend Alcorn Agricultural & Mechanical College. My complaints and negative opinions of past teachers no longer seemed relevant. I felt quite the contrary. I suddenly understood the magnitude of what each teacher had done for me, pushing different parts of me to develop the various skills I needed to bring me to this point. I hated Mrs. Jackson during my first year of high school and thought she was rude and evil. Now, my opinion of her shifted and I saw how loyal and deeply committed to her students' success she was. I even understood how it must have felt for Mr. Weddington, my old elementary teacher, to carry the weight of each of his student's success on his shoulders, especially given the tumultuous times in our small community.

The first few days in college provided a source of relief for me. However, as days went by and I prepared for my courses, I realized I was gaining new tasks and challenges for my future. Being in college carried with it a huge responsibility. I too, bore weight on my shoulders—the weight of my family's dreams and goals.

With this new opportunity, I could afford to meet and greet new people. I got to experience a wide range of students from different cultural backgrounds and disparate origins. As a Negro, it surprised me that I was both encouraged and disillusioned in this new environment. There was a new social behavior woven into this unfamiliar society, both unpleasant and admirable.

In the following weeks, I spoke with my parents about the positive and negative personalities I encountered. They were enthused to have an open dialogue about the mores of people. They advised me to choose college peers with the same character, same ambitions, same moral standards, and same study traditions that I possessed. As time passed, I appreciated that attending high school here on campus had indeed helped me develop an acuity for discernment. I followed my parents' advice.

As my parents wished, the first semester enabled me to choose classmates that had similar goals. My parents and I developed some objectives to succeed in achieving my goals. My freshmen advisor was invaluable in providing knowledge on what courses to register in. In my leisure time, I became enamored with college sports, especially football and basketball. I was caught up in the college spirit, cheering our teams on to victory. Of course, the rest of college life—

concerts, lyceum lectures, and discussions—was also stimulating.

I had initially enrolled in general studies because I had no idea what to major in. It felt as if I were searching for an answer from "the ghosts" of those hallowed halls. As college life evolved, near the end of the first semester, I spoke with Daddy often for his help in choosing a major.

In some ways, because of all the veterans on campus, I was subconsciously forced into a wider scope of events. One such veteran, Medgar Evers, displayed genuine character and a talent for leadership. He served as an Army Sergeant and fought in the Battle of Normandy in June of 1944. He had the temperament and desire to help others by shattering the walls of Jim Crow. His objectives were to bury the racism and hatred conceived by Whites and divert his energy into forming a uniformed society of respect, enchantment, and affection. He believed by erasing this venomous segregation and discrimination, the halls of injustice would roar and plummet eternally. I admired his fortitude, tenacity, and clever brinkmanship.

In my second semester, my parents and my faculty advisor suggested I consider taking subjects that would lead me on to dental, medical, or law school. Daddy gave me the nickname "Question Box" when I was younger because I asked so many why, when, and how questions throughout my elementary and high school career. Law school seemed like a good choice for me. As Daddy put it, "Eugene, I think you would make a great lawyer. You ask a 'why' question and want the answer immediately." To me, however, the thought of pursuing a law education was far-fetched and uninteresting. After some fastidious thinking, I concluded that I should carry on with agriculture and get a degree in that, since the family was immersed in farming. Daddy and Mr. Dunbar, the county agricultural agent, were happy with my decision, although my parents reiterated that their first choice was either pre-dental, for a Doctor of Dental Surgery (DDS) degree, or pre-med, for a Doctor of Medicine (MD) degree.

The general courses in agriculture during my second semester were appealing. They taught me the theory behind soil readiness, incubation of plants, and farm production. The course in general chemistry intrigued me by enabling me to understand soil analysis and plant tissue analysis. This experience permitted me to share and practice the theories at home on our farm. I was able to perform calculations for terraces and make designs for water conservation and land erosion. Providing our family with lessons from my classes felt like God was guiding me to show my parents my appreciation for their sacrifices. The school year progressed rapidly as I applied the knowledge I gained from college to better our farm techniques.

Immediately after my freshman year, the Korean conflict started. Daddy lectured me to remain high on the Honor Roll. He wanted me to apply to dental or medical school by taking the entry tests at Meharry Medical College in Nashville, Tennessee. He advised me that dental and medical students were being granted deferred statuses, which would prevent me from being sent to the front lines in Korea. I totally disregarded his advice; I figured I knew what was best for me. Now, at age 17, I believed I was invincible and had no desire to end up in Nashville. I returned to the farm for the summer and continued my regular farm activities. However, since I was not happy or impassioned with the summer work, high humidity, and extreme temperatures, the classroom seemed a glorious path to take and I couldn't wait to oblige.

I joined my classmates to welcome our sophomore year in 1950. This same year went down in our family history as a banner year because Rosia joined me on campus for her freshman year. All of us were so thrilled for her, but for Mother Dear it meant so much more. Rosia was her first daughter. She and Rosia shared so much. Mother Dear had poured every bit of herself, her dreams, and her efforts into making sure that Rosia was well-equipped for this day. Mother Dear was beaming with pride. I was happy to help shepherd Rosia through the maze of red tape in the registration process, getting her acclimated to campus life while avoiding some pitfalls. This time, she too, got to experience the transition from high school student to college student.

Rosia had decided to major in English. She found her advisor and registered for her classes, as did I. As the first semester advanced, the importance of being responsible in achieving success was becoming more and more clear to me.

Another new student joining Rosia for her first year on campus was Myrlie Beasley. She enrolled as an education major intending to minor in music. She met Medgar Evers, who was much older than she was, on her first day. The sparks between them were immediate; they soon became inseparable on campus. It seemed she was intrigued by his civil rights activism.

Within a few days, the old college energy was recharged and I was once again a happy-go-lucky student. I realized exams were forthcoming, and I had to get serious about my goals to remain on the Honor list. I was registered in courses including economics and business, which were related to farm production. The agricultural courses were interesting, especially the classwork in chicken embryology, animal husbandry, and horticulture. As I hoped, I completed the semester on the Honor Roll.

On our farm, my family continued gardening and producing crops and livestock. Mother Dear had a special interest in growing chickens for eggs. My farming responsibilities and my college courses complimented each other. I understood the theory of farming versus the practical application of farming. It caused me to develop a keen sense of humility for our family and our farm.

Social life was becoming a part of the college spirit and I was swept up in the enjoyment with my classmates. The love of football and basketball was ingrained in our hearts, as was our main rivalry with Jackson College. Off campus, very little social life existed since the college was not located near any metropolitan area. We enjoyed going to Jackson for the games because we could end the night by visiting the local restaurants. We also enjoyed

93

attending college dances on the Jackson campus, and going to one of the nightclubs nearby. If my parents knew I had gone to a nightclub, I am sure they would have imposed restrictions on me, like denying me the use of the car or the extra money they provided.

We were all enjoying campus life— balancing academic responsibilities with sports and social events—and the rise in activism. The second semester allowed me to think more independently about my ambition and whether or not I would pursue farming as a profession. My professors seemed to take a special interest in my academic achievement, knowing that Daddy was a pastor in the community. I think they felt compelled to keep him informed of my progress. Dr. J.D. Boyd, my math professor, had an interesting encounter with me on the campus lawn one day. He chastised me for not exerting my fullest potential and threatened to inform my parents. He kept his promise and did eventually inform them. My other professors alerted my parents as well when I did not perform up to my full ability.

During the spring of 1951, I joined the Omega Psi Phi fraternity. The fraternity was exemplary in both scholarships and academics. All the members inducted were honor-roll students and relied upon each other for academic support. I was inspired to excel in my subjects for the rest of the school year. My brothers and I encouraged each other to become involved in student government leadership roles. All of the fraternities and sororities were united in their efforts to make college life enjoyable.

The semester ended with me on the honor roll, even though I did not fully apply myself in my coursework. Over the summer, I was consumed, once again, with the same farm responsibilities as previous years, hauling cotton to the gin in Port Gibson and carrying other farm products to the markets. Our farm machinery had been updated, which reduced the manual labor. The field hands, males and females, continued taking on the important tasks of farming, sacrificing their time and health in the harsh conditions.

After several years, Mother Dear convinced Daddy to build a home for Big Mama to be near us. Big Mama's health had begun to fail due to a long history of diabetes and inadequate medical treatment. She could no longer perform her duties in the Galloways' home. Daddy and Mother Dear located a desirable spot on the family property to build the home. They agreed it would be a three-room cottage, larger than her servant's cottage on the Galloway plantation.

Daddy performed all the carpentry work himself to construct her home. My brothers and I, and one lone field hand, were handy helpers. Daddy taught us how to select clear lumber for its quality. He taught us not to use pieces that were not plumb, had a lot of knots that would be difficult to nail into, or had cracks or splits in the wood grain. We assisted with holding the measuring tape at one end of the lumber to make sure the cuts were accurate. We took turns passing the lumber to be cut and catching it on the other end to stack it, helping keep a good pace to the work.

We mixed the mortar for the foundation and for attaching the bricks. I observed Daddy hammering nails into the lumber. It was particularly interesting to witness the way he cut the 2x4 and 4x4 lumber with such precision in developing the designs for the pitch for the roof. (Of course, no children were allowed on the roof.) Corrugated tin was used as a cover for the roof.

Soon the walls were up; the windows, doors, and cabinets were installed; and the floors were finished. Big Mama was so excited to see her new home. Mother Dear was careful to pack her things for the boys to move. The girls were tasked with carefully decorating each room to accommodate Big Mama's health constraints. Big Mama was nearly 71 years old when she moved in. She was grateful to be closer to Mother Dear and felt truly at peace in her new home.

As the Fall semester of 1951 commenced, I was starting my junior year with confidence. I had begun to feel woven into the college fabric, mentoring younger students and providing assistance in any way I could. Rosia was starting her sophomore year; Harold was inducted into the family higher-education legacy and started his freshman year. The campus now had to contend with three Spencer siblings at once, just as the high school had. Daddy and Mother Dear accompanied us to our advisory sessions and made sure we enrolled in the right courses that aligned with our interests. My courses, including biology, math, and physics, were intense.

The professors at Negro colleges and universities were available daily for student consultations. They were committed to providing village-like communities to nurture and assist students with their academic endeavors. I believe slavery created special social relationships within the Negro community. To survive White oppression and injustice and to avoid being hanged, raped, and/or murdered in Mississippi and throughout the country, Negroes formed unbreakable alliances of mutual interest to navigate through the Jim Crow maze.

Medgar Evers had served as the student government president during his junior year. Now, in his senior year, Medgar organized a group of high school and college students, mostly veterans, to boycott a cleaning business in Port Gibson. He believed that the White business was overcharging the students and suggested that all students patronize the college laundry instead. The boycott was successful and raised awareness of the injustices perpetrated by Mississippi Whites. After a year of close association with Medgar, the students realized that he was indeed from another planet. He had brilliant ideas of ending segregation in Mississippi and many of the students quietly joined in his efforts. The Myrlie Beasley we knew as charming and composed was fast becoming more vocal in support of Medgar's activism. The semester ended with the news that Medgar and Myrlie had married on Christmas Eve.

Spring semester of my junior year progressed. Daddy was very much aware of the Korean War and was concerned about the number of Americans being killed. The draft numbers for Negroes were higher than Whites in Claiborne County. He pleaded with me to take the dental or medical tests to become a dentist or physician and be deferred. Again, I was arrogant and believed I was the best person to make decisions about my life. I refused to follow the path to professional school. With the influence of my agriculture professors, I declared a major in agricultural economics.

I believed that major would allow me the flexibility of obtaining a job with the United States Department of Agriculture (USDA) or owning and operating a farm of my own. By now, I had been apprised of my parents' net profits and how farming was becoming mechanized. I hunkered down on my classwork and concentrated on gaining knowledge about economics as it related to farming. Even the knowledge that farming required steady, strenuous work did not completely discourage me from the idea of owning a farm. It was mind-boggling that I was so indoctrinated into having a farm. I think, subconsciously, after observing Daddy's business acumen and approach for increasing profits, I had always wanted to take the same path. His profits were much higher than that of any college professor.

12 First to the Finish Line

My fourth year of college began with mixed emotions for many reasons. It was time to figure out my best options for life after college. It was a bit overwhelming and thrilling at the same time. There was so much going on in the family, in our small community, in the state, and in the world. Daddy and Mother Dear had gifted me with the awareness that all things were possible to achieve with a good work ethic. I thought about so many things, considering whether to follow in Daddy's footsteps and purchase my own farm or to work for an independent entity.

Daddy had inside knowledge on the number of Negro males, compared to White males, being drafted for the Korean War as he had befriended the White chairman of the Claiborne County Draft Board. (He provided the draft status of males within the county.) According to what he learned, Daddy said I would be near the top of the list after graduation. Daddy was known as the "influential colored farmer" in Claiborne County among the White business owners and banks. (Later, Daddy made history as the first Negro to serve as chairman of the Farm Co-Op in Claiborne County, among all the White racists.)

Keeping the family intact was paramount to Daddy. He was hard-pressed to keep me far away from the front lines, and he knew Harold would be facing the same situation next. Harold, now in his sophomore year, had decided to major in business administration. He was quite good on the basketball team. Rosia was starting her junior year and doing well in all her classes. Her English professors were confident that if she stayed the course, she would graduate with high honors.

My fraternity and other organizations on campus were active in bringing speakers and cultural groups to campus to enrich the student and faculty experience. My Omega Psi Phi brothers were used to the campus and social scenes. We followed the advice of our advisors and never went out alone. Hatred toward Negroes was boiling over in Mississippi with increased police brutality and increased killings.

One Saturday evening, I drove my father's new Dodge pickup truck to Vicksburg with two of my fraternity brothers. We visited the Tom Wince's Blue Room nightclub. This club hosted Negro jazz and soul-greats from around the country including Louis Armstrong, Dinah Washington, B.B. King, Fats Domino, and Ray Charles. Whites also visited the club, particularly when Louis Armstrong performed.

That night, my frat brothers consumed a drink or two, though they were not inebriated. I did not drink alcohol during those days because Daddy had warned me of the danger of drinking in Mississippi. My brothers and I left the club on Clay Street and drove to Washington Street, which led out of Vicksburg. Suddenly, I looked in my rear-view mirror and saw flashing red lights. We were curious as to why we were being pulled over because I was driving below the 25-mph speed limit. I stopped and pulled over as instructed by the White policemen. We were asked to get out of the truck and were frisked up and down. We fully cooperated with the four policemen because we feared for our lives. They inquired about our destination and I told them we were students at Alcorn Agricultural & Mechanical College. This seemed to infuriate the lead police officer who sharply replied, "You are under arrest and will be booked in jail. The other two—you may go." I told my frat brothers to let my father know I was in jail and explain the circumstances.

I was roughed up and placed on the back seat between two burly White policemen. En route to the jail, one of them punched me in the face. I did not retaliate. I began to shed a tear, praying that my life would be spared. I believe God enabled me to maintain my composure and out-think those predatory policemen. I knew if I responded with a counter-punch, I would likely be lynched before ever arriving at jail.

I told the lead officer that Daddy was a preacher and I knew the president of Alcorn Agricultural & Mechanical College, Dr. Otis. I was totally confused as to what the charges would be. At the jail, I was booked and placed in a holding tank. I requested to contact Dr. Otis and was refused. I figured mentioning him would influence them not to kill me.

I was extremely afraid in that dark, lonely cell with four, White, racist policemen foaming at their mouths with hatred. My clothes were moist from the perspiration pouring from my face and body as I hoped to escape this "holy hell" experience. In that moment, it would have been easy for me to dislike all White people in Mississippi with a vengeance, but I reminded myself of my family's teachings to love and care for all mankind.

Daddy arrived at the jail at 3:00 a.m. and paid the fine of $30. The policeman scolded my father, "Rev, you should teach this boy to be respectful." Daddy did not respond. He knew we were facing an impossible predicament; he also knew, inherently, how to deal with White people during this kind of crisis.

When I gained my freedom, I felt like the weight of the whole world was hoisted off my shoulders. I remember making a mental note for this to be my first and last such physical encounter with Whites in Mississippi. Though relieved, I did not believe this encounter would have occurred in our local community because the White Chief of Police and other officers knew Daddy well. I was very thankful Daddy had taught me to not react when confronted by Whites. It probably saved my life.

On the ride home, now nearing 4:00 a.m. on Saturday morning, Daddy spoke in a measured tone explaining how God had spared my life. He never questioned why I went to the Blue Room nightclub. He knew if I had not gone to the club, that situation would have been avoided. He also knew the impact of being ushered into jail weighed heavy on my mind. Suddenly, I was stimulated to do well in school, remembering the many hours that Medgar Evers had spent speaking against the injustices of racism, counseling us to "Be the best and pursue an education."

Medgar had graduated the previous year, claiming his rightful place, in my view, as a civil rights trailblazer. He was committed to spreading the value and power of community activism. He often spoke of power in numbers and this message came home to roost with me. My parents stood firmly by me after my crisis in jail and advised me to be confident in my ambitions.

The school year progressed in a viable way with my professors demanding my best academic effort. Dr. Benjamin Harris, my Agricultural Economics advisor, inspired me to reach for lofty heights in my major. Dr. Harris advised his students to use the guiding principles of capitalism with laissez-faire economics in agriculture. He believed in free enterprise or a market-driven economy where the farmer would benefit from greater profits. The major emphasis, for his students, was on farm ownership, producing high crop yields, and increasing profits. I was initially attracted to owning a farm, however, I had observed the obstacles Daddy had had to overcome as a sharecropper and then farm owner. Due to the rampant racism, starting from the USDA downward to the local authorities in Mississippi, I wanted no part of being a Negro farmer in America. The lack of farm parity for Negro farmers was an iniquity.

My last semester at Alcorn was wonderful, notwithstanding some difficulty with the chair of the Business Administration Department, Dr. Polly Ann White. I attended the business law course she taught. I enjoyed the class and had completed the assigned accounting problems and business law projects. Going into the final examination, I had an A-average and was confident that would be my final grade. Then Dr. White accused me of plagiarizing my classmate's paper while he caused a disturbance during the final examination. I had done no such thing.

I made an A on the final examination, but Dr. White gave me a D for my final grade of the class. I discussed it with Dr. White, explaining that I was considering dental or medical school and wanted to graduate *magna cum laude* or higher. She was emphatic she would not change my grade. I came away from our meeting angry and disappointed with her. She was a narrow-minded, tunnel-visioned, inconsiderate, evil professor.

I completed my remaining exams and met with my advisors to review my post-graduate options. My classmates and I were caught up in the excitement of the impending Commencement program. The black cap and gowns had been purchased, and Daddy and Mother Dear had helped me choose my class ring. The program was scheduled to be held in the Oakland Memorial Chapel. When the day arrived, our family dressed up as if we were going to Sunday services. We loaded into two cars and made our way to campus.

I hugged Mother Dear and proceeded to line up and march in with my classmates. The president of the college, Dr. Jesse R Otis, and the esteemed professors took their seats in the pulpit of the Chapel. After the "Welcome" speech and introductions, Dr. Otis gave his heartfelt thanks to our guest speaker, Dr. Benjamin E. Mays, the president of Morehouse College. Dr. Otis then gave a brief biography of Dr. Mays, who had held his position as president for 13 years. He had joined the faculty of Morehouse College as a mathematics teacher and debate coach, and had earned a master's degree and PhD from the University of Chicago.

The other graduates and I were overjoyed. Dr. Mays stood, shook hands with Dr. Otis, and made his way to the podium. Dr. Mays gave our class a vision of hope, dreams, integrity, and goals, with several notable quotes. I remember him standing tall, overlooking the graduates and speaking without notes. He was a giant who elevated his stature through his command of words uttered with semantic eloquence. The quote that stuck with me most was "It isn't a calamity to die with dreams unfulfilled, but it is a calamity not to dream." After the commencement ceremony ended, we gathered in the gym for some celebratory activities.

I graduated *cum laude*, barely missing *magna cum laude*, in May of 1953. After my graduation, my entire family surrounded me with love and joy for the momentous occasion. My family allowed me some time to relax and I began to concentrate on the future. I took that opportunity to reflect on the past eight years on campus. I remembered Mrs. Jackson, my high school assistant principal, and how I first felt she had given me such a hard time and then had discovered she was actually wonderful. Her loyalty and deep commitment to all of her students exhibited true "Mother Teresa" qualities.

I thought about Medgar and Charles Evers. They certainly left a void on campus when they graduated. I missed Myrlie, too. I remembered her playing piano in our music classes. I also remembered that she had been raised by her paternal grandmother and aunt, both of whom were teachers. Suddenly, I thought about my own paternal grandmother, who died at the young age of 32. I had always respected Daddy's wishes to not discuss her. This made me appreciate that I had spent a lot of time with Big Mama when she worked for the Galloways. With her now living on the property, I could spend time with her as often as I wanted. In that moment, I appreciated, also, that many of the classmates who started this journey with me at Alcorn Agricultural & Mechanical College achieved this momentous milestone right alongside me.

Within a few days, I realized I was eligible for the draft.

13   Uncle Sam is Calling

I checked with Daddy to see where I stood for the draft. We decided not to seek information on my status because it would surely alert the draft board about my availability. I was exceedingly perplexed about the future. I knew it was just a matter of days before Uncle Sam would come calling. I decided to travel to Jackson, Mississippi during the summer of 1953 to take the examination for the entrance into the United States Air Force. I thought it would be better to choose my branch of service rather than be forced into the army. I was accepted and given military orders to fly to Lackland Air Force Base in San Antonio, Texas for basic military training.

The air force provided commercial air transportation to Texas. On arrival in San Antonio, I presented my orders to the van driver and was taken to the base for processing. After being processed with the personnel office, I received the government-issued allowance for clothing and other basic materials for recruits. I was then transported to the barbershop to have my hair shaved. The stop at the barbershop surprised me only because it was first. I was expecting to be shown the barracks first. I sat down in the chair, silently watching all of my hair fall to the floor within a matter of minutes. I wasn't really concerned about how I might look because it was over and done with quickly. It was, however, the first time I was fully aware that I would be told where to go and what to do, without anyone asking for my input. This grooming was the initial phase of the overall programming every trainee had to go through.

My next destination was the barracks, and those would serve as my sanctuary for the duration of my boot camp training. A few days after I arrived at the air base, Daddy called to inform me that the Claiborne County Draft Board had drafted me for the army and I should report immediately. I was thankful to God that I had escaped the army and was relatively satisfied with the air force instead.

I was informed I would undergo a series of examinations during my first week. Every incoming airman was given a series of tests to determine what career they would be assigned to. The tests were designed and weighted to fit the individual's aptitude with the current mission. The results were compared with other air force personnel and the airman was assigned according to his performance on the tests. I qualified for radar engineering and electronics school. I wanted to know more about the school and was told that few airmen qualified for this training, especially Negroes. I considered air cadet school but was informed that pilots and navigators were being sent directly to Korea and I would have to sign an extension of service. I did not desire to have any type of combat duty while in service. My desire was to finish my tour of duty as soon as possible and depart honorably from the air force.

Basic training at Lackland Air Force Base was six weeks of rigorous and grueling instruction. The boot camp's physical training was much more demanding than farm labor, but getting used to the military uniform, boots, and packs was not so different from plowing and planting the fields or carrying a full cotton sack at harvest-time.

My college had prepared me for competition and for tackling any challenge I encountered. College competitions tested my fortitude—fortitude that ensured I was up to the task of completing this training. I calculated the necessary physical energy for each drill while measuring my pace against that of the other trainees. I had the courage, distinction, and discipline to advance to the next level. Because I was the only Negro in the barracks and on the drill team I was driven to succeed, despite the racism and injustice demonstrated by the airmen in charge.

On weekends, I remained in the barracks, usually alone, and relaxed by reading a book or magazine or listening to music. It was a lonely environment because the White airmen did not associate with the Negro airmen and there was no place, on or off the base, I felt comfortable exploring. I chose to stay on the base because the White civilian population was antagonistic toward Negroes. I kept myself occupied by shining my shoes and sprucing up my uniforms and cubicle. Inspections were frequent, both announced and unannounced, and if you did not pass the inspections, you were given demerits. Several demerits required you to appear before the commander or appropriate personnel. You were given extra duties, such as guard duty or kitchen police duty, which included washing dishes in the dining halls. Racism was alive—only Whites were in positions of authority; most of the services were disproportionately performed by Negroes. My goal was to be immaculate in my appearance and to demonstrate leadership qualities in my character. It was my goal to illustrate to the White hierarchy that a Negro could perform as well or better than his White peers.

All trainees got extensive training with firearms. Understanding and practicing the rules for the safe handling of military-grade weapons was intense—you knew your life, or someone else's, was totally dependent upon the accurate assembling, disassembling, cleaning, and repairing of guns. That training was the ultimate lesson in faith in your fellow man. Each airman in the unit had to trust themselves and all of us. We were trained to think, act, and move together. We learned the proper hand signals and fighting techniques. We crawled through water, mud, and sand in preparation for chemical, biological, and security breaches.

Near the end of boot camp, our squad was required to bivouac one evening to experience some actual combat. We were transported to a marked battleground area and given live ammunition. As I crawled through water with a full backpack, live shots were fired overhead. We were told not to stand up or we would suffer the consequences. I was very frightened because the ammunition was fired by White airmen and these same airmen did not respect the rights of the Negro airmen. Some experiences, both large and small, test your resolve in life-altering ways.

Growing up in the midst of lynchings and murders had a way of teaching you respect for your surroundings. You intuitively looked over your shoulders to identify friend from foe. Sitting in that jail cell solidified my understanding of consequences: I could have been killed had I hit that police officer back. As the lone Negro airman in my unit, I was suddenly faced with having to coalesce with White airmen. I had to work harder, study longer, and outwit each opponent at his own game. Finally, my six weeks were completed, and I was given orders to attend the radar school at Keesler Air Force Base in Biloxi, Mississippi.

I wondered why my basic training was relatively short and had not realized I had been assigned to the top radar operations, engineering, and electronics school in the air force. I was unhappy about this assignment because it meant I would be going back to my home state. I wanted to get out of the south, period! My stay in Texas came to a bitter end. I was angry and disappointed. The air force gave me a two-week furlough between assignments and I was delighted to visit my parents to rest, recover, and take a pause from my mistreatment by air force personnel.

The travel from Texas to my parents' home via a Trailways bus was an absolute nightmare and disgrace. I, a United States Air Force airman, in uniform, representing America, did not have a decent meal or adequate restroom facilities. My physical stamina and endurance were tested. I was told Negroes were required to sit in the rear of the bus and to get up when Whites needed their seats. I was forced to stand for hours, from San Antonio, Texas to Jackson, Mississippi, clinging to a support to brace myself on the moving bus. I will never, ever forget the severe physicality of having to adjust my grip and stance to withstand every bend in the road and every stop along the way, careful not to encroach upon any of the seated passengers. I crashed completely for a couple days once I arrived home.

I thought about my duty at Lackland, especially the evenings in the barracks. I told Daddy and Mother Dear that it felt as if I were completely isolated from society because most of the airmen were White racists from all over the country who shared the same hatred of Negroes. I was aware of how I would be received as the only Negro in the barracks, but I got a unique insight into how the White airmen perceived suddenly being forced into an integrated environment overnight. They assumed all of the barracks would be segregated. Only one White airman conversed with me in an amicable way, showing some modicum of empathy for my unfortunate circumstance as the lone Negro airman among 40 or more White airmen.

Daddy gave updates on family events and farm products. He had continued to lease more land. Harold and Delano had taken responsibility for getting the field hands to and from the farm and getting the products to the gin. Daddy and Delano were set to join Rosia and Harold at Alcorn Agricultural & Mechanical College that fall. Rosia would be starting her senior year, Harold would be starting his junior year, and Daddy and Delano would begin their first year. Rosia and Harold would be on hand in case Daddy and Delano needed anything.

Rosia planned to meet with her advisors to determine whether she would pursue a master's degree or PhD after graduation. Harold had the draft looming overhead. He hoped to stay away from the front lines of the Korean War. At home, Mother Dear and the girls spent extra time with Big Mama, whose health continued to decline. Big Mama was happy to see me, and I snuggled gently into my favorite spot for one of her famous hugs.

I got news that Medgar Evers was continuing his activism in the Civil Rights Movement after graduating. The United States Supreme Court had just made the ruling on Brown v. the Board of Education. Medgar challenged the segregation of the state-supported University of Mississippi by applying to law school there. He was denied admission. He continued to work for voting rights, economic opportunities, and access to public facilities for Negroes.

It was good to be home, but my time was drawing near to report to Keesler Air Force Base. I was not looking forward to traveling once again on the segregated Trailways bus. Mother Dear spent extra time preparing many of my favorite foods for the trip back to the air force. My first encounter with the same racist behavior began in Jackson, Mississippi, just where it had ended two weeks earlier. The driver of the bus, who was loading the luggage of the White passengers, refused to load my military bag in the lower compartment. He refused to handle anything from a Negro passenger. I had to place my luggage in the compartment myself. I was in uniform and had to move to the back of the bus or risk being arrested for trespassing in the front.

Once again, as White passengers filled the bus, other Negroes had to move to the back or stand. The snack my mother prepared for me was a life saver on this trip; Jim Crow regulations prevented Negroes from having a decent meal, even one who wore the uniform of the United States of America and was trained to protect the very citizens benefiting from discrimination and injustice. I stood on the bus somewhere between Hattiesburg and Biloxi. After my arrival in Biloxi, I boarded a segregated city bus going to Keesler. After passing through the gates of the base, the bus was no longer segregated and I was able to occupy the front seat. I showed my frustrations over this systematic mockery that contributed to second-class citizenship for Negroes, which upset the White bus driver. I quickly dismissed his flagrant display of disapproval and left him to his own psychological problems.

14 Welcome Back to School

I arrived at Keesler Air Force Base, reported to the base personnel office, and was processed for the ground radar electronics squadron. Keesler was one of the premier technical training centers in the U.S. Air Force. I was still unaware I had been accepted to the top school for ground radar and airfield systems. The first three weeks were eye-opening as I gradually acclimated to a new academic environment. Once again, I was the only Negro in the class. It was going to be a tall order for a young Negro from Mississippi to integrate into another close-knit group of bright, brilliant Whites.

I discovered that the class was a haven for rich, White, college-aged males evading the army draft, who were known as the "army dodgers" in air force circles. Many of my White classmates had degrees, or were near completing degrees, in mathematics, physics, engineering, and chemistry. It was as if I were stuck in a dream of unending consequences, from every direction, that I could not comprehend. I was overwhelmed because I never knew what to expect from the instructor or the students in class and the lab. I accepted the challenge, as a proud Negro, to master the subject matter and complete the course successfully. The killer instinct had become part of my consciousness. I visualized the end result as a "mountain of success" and truly believed that I would achieve my desired outcome.

I spoke with Daddy and Mother Dear and they both encouraged me to "finish the mission." During my first few months of school, I studied nightly, for four to six hours, preparing for the assignments. Since most of the students had backgrounds in science, technology, engineering, and mathematics, my degree in agricultural economics, with no background in the hard sciences, put me on an unequal playing field. Radar school was difficult initially.

To help me compete and progress with the class, the library became a huge source of inspiration and knowledge for me. I reviewed physics, chemistry, algebra, trigonometry, calculus, and statistics daily. School was day and night for the first few months of the course. My determination to survive centered on the pride and dignity my parents and former teachers had instilled in me. By coincidence, one evening, at an off-base nightclub for Negroes, I met a civilian fraternity brother who was an instructor in the upper division of radar electronics. He shared his experiences with me and volunteered to assist me with my course studies, especially the laboratory work.

We spent the evenings reviewing math, physics, chemistry and diagramming electronic circuits with resistors, capacitors, tubes, transformers, inductors, circuits, transistors, diodes, and other components. Our calculations were applied through Ohm's Law and other methods including current flow, voltage, radar, radio frequencies, resistance, transmissions, and radiation. I used my frat brother as a sounding board on my lab work and theory since I had no one else to explore the assignments with. I graduated from the first course and advanced to the upper division. With his help, I was confident I would be the only Negro to finish the course. I relaxed more and envisioned moving on to my next tour of duty.

As more free time became available, my White classmates went to beautiful Whites-only beaches in Biloxi. As a single Negro airman, there was absolutely nothing for me to enjoy socially during the day. It was actually illegal for me to go onto the beaches, and I was not inclined to risk being jailed under any circumstances. The base recreational halls were safer for me and other minority airmen. I became a decent pool player while making new friends and alliances. When I wasn't playing pool, I was in the library on weekends, working to maintain my standing in the course. I also enjoyed attending concerts featuring some of the greatest jazz musicians including Louis Armstrong, Lionel Hampton, and Duke Ellington. The base commander allowed a few Negro civilian women to attend the concerts, just to socialize with the Negro airmen. However, the events were mostly attended by White airmen and their female counterparts.

My upper division training moved along into 1954. An orientation seminar aroused my suspicion about where I would be stationed for my next tour of duty. There were no assurances about one location or another. My primary plan was to escape from the south's oppressed, Jim-Crow atmosphere. At this point, I began to construct miniature radar models, radios, and transmission sets. Understanding the frequencies of these gadgets made it easier for me to relate to the theories taught in our courses. In addition, I obtained top secret clearance in the cryptographic analysis of radar transmissions for purposes of jamming transmissions. The encryption protocols,

I believe, were only given to select classmates. I was approved to have this top-secret clearance and designation. I appreciated it; the clearance would be invaluable for my future assignments.

The day of graduation was near, and my excitement could not be controlled. It was paramount, at this juncture of my training, that I concentrate on everything required for the final exams and lab work, in hopes that graduation would be an underground exit from Mississippi. I graduated from radar school without fully comprehending I had actually graduated from such an élite school. It was well-known that many previous graduates landed high-demand civilian positions in the air force or the defense department after completing their tours of duty. My tour of duty at Keesler ended and I was given a two-week furlough before reporting to Fort Dix Army/McGuire Air Force Joint Base in Trenton, New Jersey. From there, I would move on to a radar outpost at Gander Air Force Base near St. Johns, Newfoundland.

I was happy to visit my family. It was good to see Daddy and Mother Dear and catch up with my siblings. I loved to still see the same warm smile on Big Mama's face through the wrinkled skin shaping her face and neck. Her hands were weaker as she raised them to open my favorite nesting spot, both of us wiping tears away and smiling as I snuggled into place. Rosia proudly proclaimed her place as the second Spencer sibling to graduate from Alcorn Agricultural & Mechanical College, and the first to graduate *magna cum laude*. We were all so very proud of her.

By the fall semester of 1954, Harold was starting his senior year, hoping to stay out of the war. Delano was starting his freshman year. Now that the farm business was running efficiently with managers and additional field hands, it was the optimal time for Daddy to join his boys in college. This didn't seem undoable; Daddy was already pretty proficient in balancing the demands of the farm with the demands of preaching at four churches.

After catching up on the family news, I reflected on my military achievements thus far. I was proud that I had continued to carry myself with the same dignity and integrity I learned from Daddy and Mother Dear, and I was happy they were proud of me, too. I was thankful I had just graduated from school in the same place the famed Tuskegee Airmen—a squadron of Negro military pilots in World War II—were trained. In the remaining days of my furlough, I also reflected on my future. What would I do with my life after my tour of duty? I was delighted to consider furthering my education. I outlined a financial plan to subsidize my education upon separating from the air force. The two weeks spent with my family ended too soon. It was time to make my way on to my next assignment.

15 On to Gander Via McGuire

I traveled by train from Jackson, Mississippi to New Brunswick, New Jersey. From Jackson to Washington D.C., the train was segregated for Negro soldiers and civilians alike. Overnight sleeping facilities were not accessible to Negroes and the food, all leftover meals not eaten by the Whites, was awful. Mother Dear knew Negroes were discriminated against on all means of transportation, so she prepared a large brown bag of food for me that included her fried chicken, sandwiches, cookies, and other goodies. After leaving Washington, I relaxed in an air-conditioned coach and was served a delicious meal by the staff. The Negro staff were overly courteous because I told them I had come from Mississippi and was on my way to Newfoundland. They were very aware of the injustices our people had suffered from southern Whites.

I reported to Fort Dix Army/McGuire Air Force Joint Base in Trenton, New Jersey in the fall of 1954. I departed the naval station in New Jersey on a troop transport ship bound for St. Johns. The ship was loaded with personnel representing the air force, navy, and army. One morning, I was awakened early and ordered to assist in cleaning the deck and performing kitchen police duty. I completed the tasks and when the time arrived, I left the ship near St. Johns and was driven to Gander Air Force Base to be processed for the radar outpost on the Atlantic coast.

With my processing complete, I boarded a small sea-going airplane and landed on the coast near the outpost. When landing, the pilot miraculously missed a large log. He said, "What a blessing." I was the only one to disembark at that station. I was picked up from the water in a small canoe-like vessel and taken ashore. I presumed communication from the base's headquarters was outstanding because I was greeted by air force personnel in a very timely manner. They transported me to the radar site on a huge snow truck, as light snow was everywhere. I had been advised at Gander to wear my heavy parka and snow boots. As we drove, everything was awesome to see.

The driver and I entered the compound and I was speechless. It was a drastic change for a Negro from Mississippi. At that moment, I understood why it was only a one-year tour of duty—it was freezing cold and there was snow everywhere. The station functioned as a Ground Control Intercept (GCI) and warning station, housing the 226 Aircraft Control and Warning Squadron. There were 50–70 airmen stationed at the complex, which was fully self-sustaining.

After orientation and processing, I settled in for a meal and decided to retire for the evening. My commander gave me a day off to rest and recover from my travel. I was very appreciative of his courtesy. The next day, I was briefed by my immediate supervisor on the mission and my job description and instructed to report for the midnight shift. I reported promptly at midnight and relieved the swing shift radar tech. He wasn't cordial at all. Since this was my first assignment, I expected him to welcome me to the "real" air force, but by then, my experiences in Mississippi had subconsciously programmed me to also expect Jim Crow racism.

I reviewed the operating manuals for the radar sets. The MPS-7, a massive search radar antenna, was mostly used for range and detection, and the height radar finder was mostly used for altitude and detection. The radar site was classified as top secret and was part of the Distal Early Warning System (DEW)—a chain of air force radar sites stretching across the Arctic Circle developed by the United States and Canada. The purpose of the early warning system was to monitor Russian fighter planes and bombers encroaching Canadian and American air space. The Russian Bear Bombers were a nuclear threat to the U.S. Upon detection, U.S. fighter planes were sent from Gander or Goose Bay Air Force Base to intercept any unfriendly aircraft.

This required the radar sets to operate 24/7 and the technician on duty was totally responsible for their operation. Our site was located out on the peninsula in an area of strong winds. My supervisor warned me that the site had lost radar sets from high winds. The pressurized domes enclosing the radar sets had failed and the sets ended up in the ocean. Since I had to physically monitor the radar sets within the dome periodically, it was challenging and scary. When the wind howled it was unnerving; I wondered if I would end up in the ocean, too.

I was accountable for monitoring the pressurized domes on an oscilloscope in the operation room, surrounded with multiple scopes and radar test equipment that made it look like the deck of an alien spacecraft.

Numerous books and manuals were available in the office for me to review, which I did often. If a radar equipment failure occurred, I was able to troubleshoot the problem immediately and have the radar sets back up and transmitting the desired frequencies for jamming, transmission, detection, navigation, and altitude. No classified information related to cryptographic analysis was ever discussed or documented in any non-classified fashion. At the end of the shift, thorough reports were completed for the incoming radar technician.

Naturally, since I was the only Negro, I believed the reports required my best efforts. I did not have anyone to confidentially discuss the "ins and outs" of the radar operation with. Maybe I was overly cautious because of my experiences at Keesler. At any rate, because of the proclivity for racism, I had no alternative but to struggle alone.

A small village of Canadians were nearby, approximately two miles down in the valley. The locals were very friendly and treated the airmen wonderfully. This was my first real experience with White people who seemed to truly have no racist agendas. I was able to establish new relationships with many wonderful and friendly people. Even the females were extraordinarily friendly and did not show any racist attitudes. For the first time in my life, I did not experience any racial discrimination in my day-to-day activities. It was astonishing to me. Here, the fellow troops treated each other with great respect and dignity. Being in Canada changed the racist attitudes of the airmen and created close relationships. Isolation from American society in a foreign country also created an environment in which Americans all clung together.

The winter weather was vicious—five to six feet of snow and ice and very high winds. Snow and ice covered the windows, creating the illusion of 24 hours of darkness. Snow plows were used to clear roadways for the delivery of supplies. I think it was the weather that convinced me to enroll in the University of Maryland Extension Course Plans. The air force paid for me to continue my education. Geopolitics and Paleontology were two subjects that piqued my interest. My studies provided me with a period of time to delve into deep thoughts. My final grade average was an A.

The radar sets were maintained well. One evening, an unidentified blip showed up on the Plan Position Indicator (PPI) scope on my screen. The control officer requested a jamming plan, which was well executed. U.S. Air Force fighter planes scrambled, and Russian aircraft departed our air space. Mission accomplished!

The air force dentist from headquarters visited our site twice during my tour of duty in Newfoundland. He had graduated from the College of Dentistry at the University of Michigan. We talked during his first visit and our discussion led me to inquire about becoming a dentist. He was receptive and supportive, sharing the pros and cons from his experience. Our discussions had a profound effect on me and I began to actually consider dental school. This was another new experience for me—a White man took special effort to advise me about a potential career path. During his second visit, we chatted again about dentistry and he encouraged me to consider dentistry as a profession; he even extended his assistance. I was so appreciative for his wise words of encouragement. Of course, I could not help but reflect back on conversations I had with Daddy before I graduated college in which he suggested I attend dental or medical school.

As with the dentist, when the physician visited our site, he encouraged me to consider medical school. These men demonstrated the highest degree of character for all of humanity, regardless of race. These men, who shared their wisdom, virtue, and righteousness with a young Mississippi native, created a new awareness in me. I saw firsthand that my color really didn't matter to them.

As the year passed, I thought about my stateside tour of duty. I inquired about not being stationed in the south, but I knew the air force would not respond. I had a casual acquaintance with an attractive, Canadian, female nursing student and she wanted to know if she could visit me in the States after she graduated. I was not interested in having a serious relationship with her and I knew it was not safe to have a White female visit me in the States. She accepted my answer and appreciated my honesty.

My tour in remote Newfoundland was coming to an end and I looked forward to re-entering civilization. Because of the secrecy of the mission, the airmen were mostly confined to their quarters and had limited contact with the outside world. The only civilians allowed on site were technical support, though I can recall only one or two civilians who rendered technical advice. Working the midnight shifts made me feel even more isolated. My departure date arrived and as I descended into the valley to board the small boat on the Atlantic Ocean I looked back at the site. I had an eerie feeling as I boarded the small sea-going plane taking me to Goose Bay Air Force Base. It was surreal seeing the radar site gleaming off the snow-capped mountain as we ascended over the mountain top.

I joined two other radar techs aboard the plane who were going back to the States. We arrived at Goose Bay and I thought we landed in another world. The troops were well-shaven with pressed uniforms, fresh haircuts, and shined shoes. They were very military-like, yet very courteous. I think they felt sorry for us because we looked like aliens from another planet in our dress and demeanor. I was led to a private room in the barracks and instructed to relax as I needed, whether to shower or sleep, and to use the dining hall next door. After some rest and recovery, I made my way to the dining hall and consumed a scrumptious meal. After, I retired for the evening and worried about my next assignment, still hoping to not be stationed in the South. I was consumed with thoughts of another encounter with "Mr. Jim Crow." I was sick of the constant racial injustices.

The next day I was processed and given orders for a radar station in North Carolina at Fort Fisher Radar Station near Wilmington. I was disappointed I was not assigned up north or in California because of the prejudice and racism in the South. Racism and discrimination were present in other parts of the country, but they were not as violent and cruel as they were in the South.

The airmen were advised to fly from Goose Bay wearing arctic uniforms, just in case the aircraft went down in the arctic weather. As I observed the terrain of snow-capped mountains, it occurred to me that if the aircraft crashed, my chance of survival was slim. I prayed I would connect with my parents and siblings once again.

It was very warm upon my arrival at McGuire Air Force Base in New Jersey. I was escorted to a private room in the barracks immediately. The same service was provided as at Goose Bay. New uniforms were issued, primarily for the humidity and heat in New Jersey and also for going south. While at McGuire, I upgraded my appearance and military decorum by going to the barbershop and having my uniforms pressed. It was great to be back in the real air force, ready to assume my mission as an airman.

Soon I was off to Mississippi for a visit with my family. My last visit seemed like a lifetime ago. Now 23, and having been out of the United States for the first time, so much had changed in me. I decided to take a train from New Jersey to Washington, D.C. and to fly from Washington to Jackson, Mississippi. The thought of having to experience just one second of racist acts aboard the train or bus was more than I could bare. To be crammed into the back seat or forced to stand for hours, unable to eat or to use the restrooms on-board or in the stations, was such a disgrace to the uniform of the United States Air Force I was wearing. In some stations, Negroes were treated worse than animals, not even allowed to have water. Sometimes people would sell cold sandwiches and soda from a back window, but there was no guarantee what they had put in it. What were clean, air-conditioned, and comfortable compartments for Whites were soiled, broken compartments for Negroes. There was no air conditioning and the compartments were near the coal engines, where coal dust and debris made you choke in the summer heat. I had just served this country for a year, in a remote outpost, to prevent a nuclear attack. It was offensive, and the height of ignorance, for a soldier to be welcomed back to this country under a cloud of racism and oppression. It was definitely safer for me to fly to Jackson.

The visit with my family was extraordinary and quite relaxing. I was happy to be a civilian for two weeks and to see how much of the farm had been automated. I was also happy to learn that farm production was high. I even got to spend some time with Harold and Delano fishing at the pond and creek near the house.

Rosia had graduated the previous summer and Harold had just graduated a few weeks earlier. Delano and Daddy had completed their freshman years and both were set to graduate in 1958. My biggest excitement was when my mother revealed that she was on schedule to start college the next year, in 1956, at the same time as Doris. This was wonderful news! They would graduate together in 1960, finally completing the long-held legacy of all of our family receiving college degrees. This was priceless and history in the making.

16 The Racist Side of Being Stateside

During my two weeks of rest and recovery at home, the travel from Mississippi to North Carolina raised concerns for my safety. I did not have the patience or will to be confronted with hateful, racist White people. I was just done! I made my way to Wilmington, North Carolina as best I could. The trip did not include any stops because Negroes were not allowed to stay in any hotels. I had been ridiculed from back doors and alleyways all across the South. Once again, even though I was a United States Air Force airman in uniform, serving my country, its own citizens did not recognize my existence.

An air force van transported me from Wilmington to the Fort Fisher Radar Station. It was an obvious contrast from my last post. Processing by the radar station personnel was anything but cordial. The airmen were stiff and inhospitable with each other, so it was no surprise how they treated a newcomer like me. My newly assigned supervisor, a burly sergeant, did not have a welcoming disposition either. The site had four to six radar techs manning the facility and again I was the only Negro. I hoped to see more people of color coming in the next wave of assignments so I would have someone to collaborate with in our daily briefings.

Since this was not the case, I attended college again and the air force paid the fees. I enrolled in Wilmington Junior College. The air force allowed me to drive a free van for transportation to class. I took a refresher course in chemistry, which allowed me to experiment with plastics and materials in the laboratory. The electronic circuits of the radar sets seemed to have an inordinate amount of plastics, which may have been an assumption on my part. I aced the course, earning an A for the final grade.

Fort Fisher was located out on a peninsula on the Atlantic coast. The location, near beautiful Kure beach, was breathtaking. Negro airmen were barred from Kure beach, hotels, and restaurants, so the seven or eight Negro airmen on base had few places to go, or things to do, after duty.

The beach was a paradise for White airmen. One such airman, Rudd, from Minnesota, tried on more than one occasion to entice me to join him and his girlfriend on the beach. Rudd was acquainted with the Jim Crow laws of North Carolina and the nation, but truly tried to help me and comfort me on and off the base. Rudd sacrificed time he could have spent at the beach, restaurant, and clubs, frolicking among his White friends, to shoot pool and play other games with the Negro airmen. He extended his sincere, deep convictions about the injustices toward Negro airmen but was helpless to resolve the social disorder. He was honorably discharged shortly after I arrived. I believe he went back to Minnesota with his bride.

Sea Breeze, a small beach that catered to Negroes, was a few miles from Fort Fisher. During the week, a few people came to the beach. There was the usual very loud music from mounted speakers. The businesses were largely mom-and-pop joints; there were no nice hotels or fine-eating establishments. Simply stated, it was just a pebbly shore without any classy facilities.

On weekends, the place overflowed with people. They strolled the streets and the beach, seemingly having an exuberant time. It was a melting pot for Negroes and a place to "let go" for a little while, away from the oppression caused by a racist society.

I received a promotion and the base commander spoke with me about making a career in the air force. My response was blunt. Assignments in the South were so demoralizing for Negroes and without any control over my duty assignments, it was not feasible for me to make a career in the air force. The commander listened as I explained my position and clearly understood my perspective. As the end of my air force duty neared, I implemented the maintenance of the radar sets with diligence and dedication. I had given this country my best, protecting the shores from a nuclear or surprise attack. The opposite was true for most people of color. The United States did not protect us from the demons of Jim Crow and the racism and injustices sewn into the inner fabric of America.

Six months before the end of my tour of duty, I decided to pursue dentistry or medicine and I applied to Howard University. With only a month left in the air force, I went home to drive Daddy's car back to North Carolina to be able to transport my belongings upon separation. Eventually, the day of reckoning came. I drove to Pope Air Force Base, which was adjacent to the Fort Bragg Army Base in North Carolina. The two bases combined to form one of the world's largest military installations. This was determined to be the location of my final separation. In 1957, I was given an honorable discharge from the United

States Air Force and four years of GI educational benefits.

I mapped the safest route to get home using the major highways. There were few places for Negroes to lodge overnight in the Negro neighborhoods of Atlanta, Georgia, and Alabama. I wore my Air Force uniform thinking it would add protection from southern militia, the KKK, White racists, and White cops during my trip. When I entered South Carolina via Highway 95 one early evening, I noticed my fuel was low and I got off the freeway to refuel. I approached the White attendant in the station for a refill. While he filled the tank, I haphazardly drank some water from the "White fountain" instead of the "colored fountain" because the signs were blurred.

I did not realize I had broken a Jim Crow law until he suddenly said, "BOY, stop drinking that water from the wrong fountain." I told him to stop pumping the gas and he became unnecessarily angry. I paid him and sped off immediately. As I got back on the freeway, I began to perspire profusely from the confrontation. My instinct was to exit the freeway quickly and go to a camouflaged area, taking advantage of my military training. Soon afterwards, there were red lights flashing from a state trooper traveling down the highway at a high speed. I remained in my camouflaged position for more than an hour. I believe the White gas station attendant alerted the state trooper about our confrontation.

My journey continued, via Interstate 20 to Atlanta, with some trepidation; GIs returning from the service and the war were being murdered by White extremists in the South. Finding a safe place to sleep became a bigger factor. I carefully chose an area to have a military snack and water, then relieved myself before getting some rest. When I arrived in Atlanta, I inquired about the Negro area and was given directions by a trusted source. I celebrated my safe arrival with a good soul-meal and an evening of deep sleep. I continued to Birmingham the next morning after breakfast. My trip to Birmingham ended with an overnight stay at the A.G. Gaston motel.

When I got home, my parents and siblings welcomed the Air Force veteran with a hearty meal and lots of affection. The next two weeks were filled with family fun as I shared memories about the air force and my family reminisced about the past four years. We talked about the future outlook for our family. We were in awe of our own accomplishments. Sadly, there were three missing from that reunion celebration. Our beloved Big Mama had crossed over a few months earlier. Her home of five years still held the remnants from her treasured life with the Galloways, as if she were still there. I really missed Big Mama. Mother Dear was doing all she could to get through her first year of college in the midst of unbearable grief. Rosia was gone— she had already entered the University of Illinois—but Doris was still at home; she was truly a strong support for Mother Dear.

Daddy and Delano were starting their senior year at Alcorn Agricultural & Mechanical College and both were scheduled to graduate in 1958. However, in March of 1957, one of Delano's previous Negro history instructors, Clennon King, incited student anger by publishing a series of articles in the *Jackson State Times*, a White Mississippi newspaper known as a segregationist publication. The articles associated the NAACP with communism and included photos of Alcorn students. The students in the photos were lured into his scheme unwittingly, thinking the photos were for the school yearbook. They responded by boycotting King's classes and demanding his dismissal from the college. The boycott spread to other classes and, at the end of the year, resulted in the firing of the university president along with the dismissal of a significant section of the student body.

Harold had been drafted into the army right after he graduated college in 1955 and was stationed at White Sands Proving Ground in White Sands, New Mexico. This was the army's military missile testing area. This was also the site of the first atomic bomb test on July 16, 1945. Harold's tour of duty was scheduled to end in 1959; we prayed for him to return home safely.

Mother Dear and Doris started their sophomore year in the fall and were scheduled to graduate in the summer of 1960. All seven family members would then have bachelor's degrees from the same institution.

We recalled the late 1930s and early 1940s when our family was mired in poverty and our parents could barely feed or clothe us. Amid all those circumstances, we were able to not just survive, but thrive. We were able to reach our goals, year after year, purchasing more land and hiring more field hands, achieving more than

Daddy and Mother Dear had envisioned. WHAT
A BLESSING!

17 What's Next for Me?

"...We have come over a way that with tears has been watered, we have come, treading our path through the blood of the slaughtered..." These words from the Negro National Anthem had, in a profound way, been the anthem of my entire family: to rise above adversity, stay the course, and give our all in every dream, every goal, and every success. Everything I needed to accomplish anything was already inside me. Howard University had given me a late date to report for summer school because of my separation date from the air force.

I had to meticulously plan my trip to Washington. I checked the train schedules, knowing that the same Jim Crow laws were still in full effect. I was familiar with, and prepared to follow, all the regulations for Negro passengers — no sleeping facilities or decent meals. However, this time, it would be different because I was a different man. I was an honorably discharged United States Air Force Negro veteran. A Negro Pullman Porter comforted me on the trip after I informed him I was from Mississippi and an Air Force veteran. Beginning in Atlanta, during the evening hours, the porter provided me with some food and a pillow to snooze on. He was a member of the Brotherhood of Sleeping Porters and was well-versed in the discrimination against Negroes practiced by the railroad companies.

This Brotherhood assisted other Negroes in the designated train car. They helped mothers with babies in particular, warming the milk and providing some essentials. These porters secretly aided Negro passengers without the knowledge of their supervisors. Their covert efforts were in full swing during the late hours before they had to begin serving the White passengers. It was an underground network of comrades, paying their blessings forward.

I arrived safely in Washington, and immediately fell prey to an unseemly taxicab driver. I discovered I was being driven far out of the way to the Howard University dormitory. This increased the fair tremendously. Fortunately, the dormitory director was standing outside when I arrived and he advised me what the approximate fair should be. The driver accepted the director's recommendation and reduced the fair by almost 50%.

The day after I arrived, I registered for graduate courses in mathematics and zoology. It was important for me to make this transition back into academia slowly, being careful not to overload myself. I also had to acclimate back into civilian behavior. It was an adjustment to move from taking orders back into free thinking. It was good to familiarize myself with the patterns of higher education and of being on a different campus in a different city, far from the South. My Air Force savings amounted to approximately $5,000 and with my GI benefits, I had planned for dental or medical school expenses. The first summer session was stellar—I achieved good grades. I enrolled in trigonometry for the second summer session, wanting a review of calculations of angles and planes, in preparation for my Dental Admission Test (DAT).

By the time the fall semester approached, I had a clear plan for achieving acceptance into dental or medical school. In September of 1957, I enrolled in advanced biology and chemistry courses. I decided not to take a Christmas vacation and to work at the central Washington, D.C. post office for the two-week break. I wanted to pad my savings for whichever professional school—dental or medical—I would enroll in. My first full year in post-graduate school was a success and it energized my ambition immensely.

Daddy and Delano graduated from Alcorn Agricultural & Mechanical College in May of 1958, raising the count to five family members completing their undergraduate degrees. Daddy obtained his degree in social science while Delano finished with a degree in history. He then went on to join the army reserves. Mother Dear and Doris finished their sophomore years successfully. Like Harold had, Doris pursued a degree in business administration. Mother Dear pursued a degree in education. Rosia continued in the master's program at the University of Illinois.

I entered my second year at Howard in the fall of 1958 with high aspirations, continuing courses in zoology, organic chemistry, comparative anatomy, and histology. During a course in comparative anatomy in which I used my hands to dissect a specimen, dentistry began to interest me. In my second semester, in 1959, I took the Dental Admission Test at Howard. I sent my applications for dental school to Howard University, Indiana University, and Meharry Medical College. I was accepted by all three universities. I chose to attend Howard.

Howard requested I take a prerequisite course in physics before the fall semester of dental school. I enrolled in summer school at American University to take the necessary physics class. I attended night school because I had a full-time day job at the Smithsonian Institute and needed the funds for dental school. I completed the physics course successfully and was declared eligible to enter the College of Dentistry in the fall of 1959. It was exactly six years after Daddy advised me to attend dental or medical school. It was glorious and an epic celebration when I informed my parents I had been accepted. Both of them shed tears and wished me success. I returned congratulatory wishes to Daddy for his accomplishment of finishing college.

I decided to have some fun and amusement with a visit to New York on a fraternity boat cruise around Manhattan, before entering dental school. I knew dental school would require immense devotion, time, and dedication. Therefore, this was a good moment to have a break before the rigors of academia began. The cruise was great and lots of fun.

As I returned to Washington, a couple of weeks before school started, I was in a serious car accident. A frat brother, a third-year dental student at Howard, was driving when he hydroplaned, ejecting me from the car onto the shoulder of highway 95. We were rushed to a hospital in Summit, New Jersey where both of us remained overnight. A surgeon placed 21 sutures in my scalp. I was blessed to survive the accident. I thanked God for saving my life and allowing me to make it to my first day of school.

My opening semester was exciting. I had the chance to meet all of my 96 classmates and I did not know what to expect. There were distinguished professors in both the dental and medical schools, all with different personalities than I had anticipated. I was rigidly indoctrinated into a group of many extremely bright, Negro students. When they were gathered in one place I sensed, from the energy in the room, that discipline was a code of behavior that determined your success from year to year in dental school.

In my first semester, in the gross anatomy class, I had the distinct honor of being taught by a famous Negro anthropologist, William Montague Cobb, MD, PhD. Dr. Cobb earned his MD from Howard University in 1929 and was the first Negro to earn a PhD in anthropology from the Case Western Reserve University in 1932. His lectures in art, anatomy, and anthropology were heart-stirring as he integrated the three disciplines together. Dr. Cobb was a member of the Omega Psi Phi fraternity and studied embryology with Dr. Ernest Everett Just, a founder of the fraternity. Being a member of Omega Psi Phi myself gave me a sense of pride, increased my confidence, and compelled me to strive for success. I could relate to Dr. Cobb, not only because we were brothers, but also because I had taken a course in paleontology from the University of Maryland while I was in the air force. I was thankful to God for the fortune and blessings that enabled me to matriculate in dental school.

Previously, I had applied for a four-year stipend from the Mississippi State Department of Education and it was now approved. I would receive a monthly check for my four years of dental school, without having to reimburse the state or practice in it. It was my understanding that Mississippi really did not desire Negroes with advanced degrees to return to the state. I believe they feared Negro uprisings and therefore paid them to not come back.

The first year of dental school was similar to the first year of medical school. Some of the prerequisite clinical courses were combined and taught by either dental or medical school professors. The combined classes included over 200 students in white coats. It was fascinating to observe such a large cadre of brainy learners. It might have been emotionally overwhelming for someone else; for me it was very defining.

In combination with the preclinical sciences of anatomy, bacteriology, pathology, physiology, and biochemistry, the dental classes tested one's artistic ability and clinical perception. Other courses in medicine, pharmacy, histology, and surgery were required. I was satisfied with the outcome of my first semester. I was so confident that I was oblivious to failure. For the Christmas vacation, I worked at the D.C. post office again along with other dental, medical, and law students from Howard. When my second semester arrived, I reminded myself that my parents had both entered college at a late age. This reflection provoked me to exceed under any circumstances.

I concluded my first year of dental school. I wanted to visit my parents for the summer, but they encouraged me to remain in D.C. to seek a job. As a veteran, I was fortunate to be employed as an extern in pathology at the Armed Forces Institute of Pathology at the Walter Reed Army Hospital. I assisted the renowned oral pathologist, United States Army Major General Surindar Bhaskar, with composing the path prints and index for his upcoming Synopsis of Oral Pathology.

In September of 1960, I was a sophomore dental student. I set out to face the challenges with grace. The sophomore year was known as the most difficult year academically. The adage was, if a student finished the sophomore year, he was already a dentist. I admit that the sophomore year tested my perseverance and my studious abilities. At this stage of my life, "Survival of the fittest" was my motto and survival my goal. The end of the year revealed I successfully completed all the requirements for advancement to the junior year. A few of my classmates did not advance to the junior year.

It was a requirement to enroll in the clinic for hands-on training with patients immediately after the sophomore year. A comprehensive treatment plan for all phases of dentistry and medicine was mandated for all students. From this point on, until graduation, I was required to attend dental school year-round.

I took a short trip home to see my family and congratulate Mother Dear and Doris for reaching the pinnacle of their education. Our family claimed the ultimate victory: every member earned undergraduate degrees from the same college our parents had planned for with the purchase of their first plot of farmland so many years earlier. We were extremely blessed!

At this time, I also visited my old college. During my trip, I challenged Dr. White regarding her decision to deny me from graduating *magna cum laude*, for which she politely apologized. Several other students complained about her attitude toward them during their undergraduate experience.

I returned to Washington, happy to test the claim that the junior year would be less challenging. In September of 1961, the third-year class convened with aspirations to become ethical and competent disciples of dentistry. The dental and medical professors were imperative in their attention to ethics. They delivered quality service to all patients, especially children. It took me back to my own childhood when Daddy was so patient with me in explaining everything he was doing. He was careful to use words I could comprehend, gentle in his tone and timbre, and made sure not to startle me or make me feel uncomfortable. Each patient required the same attention and care from me.

As the year progressed into the second semester, my mind and spirit were making the conversion into dentistry. The school year ended, and I was declared a senior. Returning for the summer clinic and my last clinical session was exciting and rewarding. I was compelled to put forth my best efforts. I knew leaving a lasting legacy would be good for both my ego and for the patients and professors.

My last year of school, in September of 1962, started with some hesitation among us students. We wondered, was this truly our last year? Were we dreaming that we had finally made it? I knew I was truly dreaming because I had met a charming, lovely, beautiful, young lady named Maude Walters. She was pursuing a master's degree at Catholic University. She had a warm aura and seemed naturally sweet with a soft personality. She was neatly dressed, and her medium-length black hair shaped her face in such a way that when she smiled, her brown eyes twinkled. She was very supportive of me being in dental school.

I invited her to attend the dental and medical students' dance during the Christmas vacation. She chose not to attend. I believed she was testing me to see if I was serious about dating her, and that she was trying to maintain her high standards. I had every intention of achieving the ultimate prize by winning her heart. She was voluptuous and shaped to match my every desire. We dated as often as our respective schedules permitted. I was enamored with her soft and sedate mannerisms, and she was so low-key that spending time with her was heavenly.

I met my second, and final, semester of dental school with hope and happiness. However, I was well aware of the grueling final exams that would be administered in the last weeks. After the examinations there was a waiting period before you were informed whether you were a candidate for the Doctor of Dental Surgery (DDS) degree. This period was the most stressful time of my entire dental education. My mental and physical stability were tested as I waited for the final results.

Finally, I received the letter from the Office of the Dean. I was very nervous and had difficulty opening it. The letter congratulated me on fulfilling all of the requirements for the DDS degree. I stood for a moment, letting the information register in my brain. I leapt on the sofa in celebration with my roommate who had received his letter that confirmed his MD degree. We celebrated that evening with our other classmates, drinking champagne together. I shared the information with my love, Maude, and she was elated for me. She added her own congratulations and promised me she would attend my graduation. I graduated in May of 1963. Maude and I celebrated after the ceremony. I learned I was accepted for an internship at the Tuskegee University Veterans Affairs (VA) hospital.

Also in 1963, in Jackson, Mississippi, my old friend and compatriot Medgar Evers was assassinated. He was murdered in the driveway of his home. My fallen hero, a great civil rights activist who had inspired me to aim for the highest celestial pathways, was gone. He was assassinated by a racist who was epically notorious for his unyielding hatred of Blacks. Medgar had become the first NAACP field secretary in Mississippi. He and his wife Myrlie fought many forms of racial injustice throughout Mississippi, including the segregation of the University of Mississippi. The couple's commitment to social change undeniably assisted in bringing down the walls of racism and hatred in Mississippi. Medgar's murder gave support for more civil rights legislation.

I was in no mood to return to the segregated South; Medgar's murder reinforced my disdain for southern Whites. I was frightened by their vengeful tactics against my people. Now I have come to realize, through my parents' teachings of love for all mankind, that there are good and wonderful people in all races.

My salary at Tuskegee VA Hospital was very minimal, so I applied for a two-year commission in the air force as a dentist. I envisioned the air force would provide me with a permanent excursion away from Jim Crow in the South.

The air force gave me a direct commission and ordered me to report to Gunter Air Force Base in Montgomery, Alabama. I was shocked by this assignment that made me return to the Jim-Crow South. I conferred with the air force recruiting office and was advised that all direct commissioned medical personnel were assigned to Gunter Air Force Base for medical orientation and there were no other base assignments available. I was promised by the Washington recruiting office that this assignment was only temporary, and I would be stationed in California or Europe. California was my first choice.

After graduation, I traveled home to visit family in Mississippi. I was eager to celebrate my professional degree (D.D.S.), especially with my beloved parents, who were extremely proud of my accomplishment. On my return to Washington, D.C., Maude and I were married in the summer of 1963 at the Canterbury House on the Howard University campus. Father Albion Ferrell, Chaplain of Omega Psi Phi, performed our wedding ceremony. A couple of close friends stood with us during our holy vows of matrimony. Father Ferrell helped us with our

146

vows. He told us that marriage was a foundation of love, sanctity, joy, sacrifice, and gratification. The beginning of our partnership blossomed on that historic day.

Maude and I traveled to Greenville, North Carolina for our wedding reception at the home of her parents. Herman and Rosalyn hosted a delightful and beautiful reception filled with friends wishing us an abundance of extraordinary love and blessings. Her family showered us with deep affection and fondness that remains with us to this day. This occasion is forever engraved in our hearts as we traverse our journey through a wonderful marriage. Notably, the cake was a multilayered work of art, covered with white candles and is still sparkling with us. Peace, love and endearment to them forever for such an amazing gift!!

18 On the Way Back to the South

The Civil Rights March on Washington on August 28, 1963 advocated for the civil and economic rights of Black Americans. The march was initially supported by leaders of the "Big Six" civil rights organizations at the time: James Farmer, from the Congress of Racial Equality (CORE); Reverend Martin Luther King, Jr. from the Southern Christian Leadership Conference (SCLC); John Lewis, from the Student Nonviolent Coordinating Committee (SNCC); A. Philip Randolph, from the Brotherhood of Sleeping Car Porters; Roy Wilkins, from the NAACP; and Whitney Young, from the National Urban League. A short time later, religious and labor interests were also included.

Medgar Evers, who had been murdered a month and a half earlier, was missing from this march. Immediately after his murder, the NAACP had given his brother, Charles, Medgar's position. Myrlie Evers had continued his efforts in civil rights; she advocated for voting rights, equal access to public accommodations, and the desegregation of the University of Mississippi.

The march occurred just before I went back to active duty after graduating from dental school. For Black Americans across the South, it was so much more than a catchy caption. It was about the indescribable injustices; senseless discrimination and blatant racism; inhuman mutilations and murders; and the lack of employment and decent wages. Although I was going back into the air force, I was compelled to participate as a Black man who continued to experience injustice firsthand in Mississippi,

South Carolina, Texas, North Carolina, and all throughout the deep South. I arose at 5:00 a.m. on August 28, 1963 and made my way downtown to join the march.

Hundreds and hundreds of buses descended into Washington, and thousands and thousands of Black people assembled at the Lincoln Memorial. There were more than 250,000 people treading in a peaceful manner, hoping to bring about freedom and jobs. The intensity of the crowd was palpable. I had never seen so many Black people moving with such synchronous precision, holding hands as if to transfer power, will, and hope from one person to the next and claiming their right to occupy this space in time. My emotions were suddenly swept up into the collective as I stood on the shoulders of my own parents, and their parents, and their parents' parents.

On that historic and momentous day, Dr. Martin Luther King's "I Have a Dream Speech" raised the conscience of the world about the injustices suffered by Black people in the United States. Dr. King said of segregation, "One hundred years later, the Negro is still languished in the corners of American society and finds himself in exile in his own land."

Later in the day, it was reported that Myrlie Evers had double-booked her schedule and was caught in traffic on her way to the Lincoln Mall from the airport, thus missing the opportunity to speak at the March. In the absence of Myrlie, Bayard Rustin, chief coordinator of the march, paid tribute to "Negro Women Fighters for Freedom." Dr. King was the last speaker.

My consciousness was filled with the solidarity and respect exhibited by the people in their march to freedom.

It was personal. It was purposeful. It was powerful. It was peaceful. I will carry this forward into future generations.

In September of 1963, I was scheduled to report to Gunter Air Force Base for medical orientation. I arrived in Montgomery, Alabama by train at approximately 11:00 p.m. The White taxicab driver refused to provide me with transportation to the base. There were two White airmen going to the base at the same time and he did not want me to ride with them. He stated that he would come back to give me a ride to the base separately. I told him I was a commissioned officer and he informed me that "this is the law in Alabama." A significant amount of time passed. I feared the taxi driver might not return or, if he did, he might threaten me on a lonely highway. Finally, I called the base and informed them of the situation.

Imagine a Black airman in Alabama, where segregation is the law, being told, in the middle of the night, that he must get transportation alone! I felt like all of my DNA, in every cell, that carried the genetic instructions for my growth and development was reminding me of the beatings and lynching by White mobs bloodthirsty for the extermination of "Negroes." Racial tensions between Blacks and Whites were at the forefront of every daily interaction, and this moment was no different. My thoughts raced uncontrollably. These Whites of the Jim Crow era, with their despicable acts, completely abdicated their civic responsibilities in protecting Black people. They even abdicated their own government-issued Black airmen. It was a total double standard and an episode of social dysfunction! Finally, the nightmare ended—an air force van was dispatched and gave me safe transportation to the base.

The next few days at Gunter included basic officer orientation; learning the uniform code and the medical mission; and an introduction to the class personnel. It was all, thus far, very informal. The two-month courses provided the medical logistics of medicine, dentistry, and nursing. A class of nurses, dentists, and physicians formed a squadron in a team effort to learn how to treat battlefield victims. Class topics, presentations, and course content were demonstrated in an informal and casual method. On the weekends, the troops intermingled freely at the officer club, dancing and having enriching conversations on world affairs and global crises.

Some White classmates even extended courtesy to the Black classmates and asked them to join them off-base in a social environment. Not a single Black airman accepted that goodwill gesture; they were afraid that civilian Whites would attack them in an integrated setting. There was no social integration of classmates off-base because of alleged mongrelizing. There was always the possibility of racists committing atrocities against the Black officers. I had been warned by previous classmates at Howard University about Gunter Air Force Base, but I was more than aware of the Jim Crow laws throughout the South, having Mississippi roots myself. I reverted to spending my free time in the base's recreational halls or library.

Triage methods for treating the injured were emphasized in mass casualties on the battlefield. My training was centered on assessing the situation quickly and focusing immediate attention on the surviving soldier. I could not fully comprehend how one was able to make a split-second decision in a combat situation about who should be prioritized for medical or dental treatment—the wrong split-second decisions could result in loss of lives. This brought on a different awareness for me. I examined many medical and dental treatments and reviewed several procedures and military policies until I was confident in treating the airmen. When graduation day came, I was full of gladness for us graduating Black airmen. There were few: only two or three of us in the class of 100.

19 Westbound

It was time to leave Gunter Air Force Base in Montgomery, Alabama. I was distraught over the idea of going to Washington D.C. by bus or train. I arranged airline transportation to avoid being subjected to the segregated injustices. I arrived back in D.C., happy to be reunited with my new bride. My orders were processed for our trip to California, and I was excited to finally be assigned to the one state I had been fighting for. We found lodging in D.C. for a few days and visited with relatives and friends.

Mother Dear's sister, who was very special to me, lived close to where we were staying. Aunt Odessa Dixon invited us over and prepared a scrumptious meal on the eve of our departure for California. She was a caring and loving aunt, and our visit with her was truly endearing for both of us. She was really concerned about having to travel 3,000 miles to our final destination. We assured her we would take every precaution to travel safely. We purchased a new car and made plans for our cross-country adventure, including setting up overnight accommodations at military installations.

We were blessed to have an overnight stay in Chicago with my youngest sister, Doris. It was refreshing to be there and introduce her to my new wife. It was lots of fun talking about our family. We also shared our experiences with some of the cruelties of living in Mississippi.

Our next overnight stay, at Francis E. Warren Air Force Base in Cheyenne, Wyoming, was indeed an experience. It was very cold, and the room was poorly lit, with only a small sheet and blanket covering the single cot. It seemed like we were the first inhabitants in a long while. We dressed warmly and cuddled through the night.

The next morning, we journeyed on to Salt Lake City, Utah and found overnight accommodations that were more suitable. We chose not to visit, or even inquire about, the Mormon Tabernacle; we had learned from the media that Black Americans were not welcomed by their congregation. We drove by the Temple and disembarked from the car long enough to view the monolith. Coming from the racist South, I wanted to elude this inhumane society. I had absolutely no desire to confront racism head-on. With a family in the making, and dreaming to be free, I wanted to look beyond the elements of injustices and head toward new aspirations for my family.

We finally crossed the state line into California. We heaved a sigh of relief, releasing the pent-up emotional baggage of racism and bigotry and inhaling the news reports that the Golden State was a panacea for the advancement of Black Americans. This advancement proved to still be elusive for us; we unexpectedly experienced overt discrimination when we sought civilian housing at McClellan Air Force Base. It was November of 1963. My orders were processed, and we were temporarily housed in the Bachelor Officer Quarters (BOQ)—the designated male quarters—for two weeks. Imagine my wife living in mostly male quarters while I worked in the dental clinic. During after-duty hours, we sought off-base housing. It was a very high priority.

Because there was no oral surgeon on staff for surgical procedures, I was assigned to the department of oral surgery in the dental clinic. As a general dentist, I performed extractions and oral surgery on base personnel and airmen transferring to Vietnam. Because Black dentists performed all of the dental procedures and did not have the pleasure of referring their patients to any specialist in the South, Howard University had to train us well in oral surgery. Jim Crow laws also discriminated against Blacks seeking dental or medical treatment in a White clinic or hospital.

Later, an oral surgeon did report to the clinic. After that, I performed general dentistry and minor surgery along with the other 12 dentists. The dental commander, Colonel Fields, forbade me to search for housing during regular duty hours, although I had made him aware my concerns about my wife living in the BOQ. I was told by a fellow dentist that Colonel Fields permitted White dentists time off to find housing. He was, in my best estimation, the most insensitive specimen I had encountered in my Air Force career thus far. He was also the principal reason why I did not consider a career in the air force when I was offered a permanent commission.

Maude and I dined at the hospital cafeteria for every meal. We became friends with the non-commissioned officer in charge of the cafeteria. He was Black and sympathized with us not being able to secure a home. He went out of his way to prepare special meals for Maude. We often remained to chat with him after consuming our meals. We felt welcome in this new air force environment. The desserts we had at the end of our conversations were scrumptious and I will not forget how eating the bread pudding increased my appetite for more. I am forever indebted to him for his kindness.

Looking for housing each day became routine. We sought housing that was just off-base because the Secretary of Defense, McNamara, had given orders to local communities near military installations not to discriminate against GIs. Even so, we were often told the house was "just rented," even when the rental signs were still on display. After two weeks, I was infuriated that so many places refused to rent to an Air Force officer and his wife. The only source to mediate this problem, I thought, was the base housing office. The housing office recommended Del Paso Heights and the Strawberry Manor neighborhoods, which were both segregated and poor—there were unpaved streets and streets without sidewalks.

Homes that were advertised as available for rent were despicable, at best, and uninhabitable. We were so angry and disappointed. We were frustrated that we could not seem to escape the Jim Crow system. Without housing, our period of time in the BOQ was extended another two weeks. Every day we tried to find a safe residence, and repeatedly we were met with opposition and dishonesty from the White agents. We discovered a pervasive problem of housing discrimination even, to our surprise, here in California. Our naïveté unfortunately faded into the harsh reality of discrimination.

On November 22, 1963, I was treating patients in the dental clinic when the news of the assassination of President John F. Kennedy flooded throughout the base. I retreated to the officer's lounge overcome by the news. Out of respect to our fallen president, and because of our consternation, the dentists were excused from duty. I made my way back to the BOQ to make sure Maude was okay. We were speechless, listening to the radio and television news coming in from all over the world. As people throughout the nation grappled to make sense of President Kennedy's murder, US fighter planes scrambled to escort the President's remains, Mrs. Kennedy, and everyone who was with them home safely. The success of that mission was paramount.

Maude and I continued to search for off-base housing, to no avail. Blacks were being denied access to housing solely on race due to the unequal protection of the government. Later, it was discovered that redlining—when financial institutions and realtors made it extremely difficult for Blacks to borrow money to purchase a home in an amiable area—was very popular in the state.

By coincidence, almost four weeks after we arrived at McClellan, a White retired air force master sergeant, who was manager of an apartment complex near the base, decided to lease an apartment to us. He said, "I am going to take a chance, or break tradition, to lease a space to you because you and your wife seem to be nice people." Earlier, I had explained to him that I was a dentist on the base. As he was retired, knowing I would be rendering emergency treatment to air force retirees may have influenced his decision.

We signed a month-to-month lease and made history as the first Black couple to move into the complex.

It was vital for us to get comfortable in our new apartment. Gena was born in the base hospital in 1964. Her birth solidified our union and created an alliance between our two families. As Gena was delivered, I wondered if Maude was experiencing the severe pain my mother had experienced during the delivery of my youngest sibling; it was a heart-breaking thought. Living on the base, we developed close ties with other military families. We were like one giant family— an entourage of closeness, togetherness, and security.

Soon, Maude and baby Gena were home and we learned how to be the best parents for her. We had the support of our whole base family. Daddy and Mother Dear were as excited for us as Maude's parents, Rosalyn and Herman, were. The military illustrated how easy it was for all ethnic groups to live in harmony on the base, yet civilians in the country continued to perpetuate discord and hatred of Black people, killing and creating injustice. The secure atmosphere and friendly community on-base prompted me to consider making a career in the air force, though it was premature to make such a decision.

A few months after living in the off-base complex, the base's housing department informed us that a home was ready for immediate occupation. Our off-base apartment was very comfortable, and we were very grateful to the White apartment manager for taking a chance on us. We confirmed that we were, in fact, nice people and he confirmed that some White people could be trusted. We left the apartment as clean as it was when we moved in and made arrangements to move into our new home. This change of residence was another happy occasion for us. For the first time, Maude and I experienced the beauty of having a home that was less burdensome than an apartment. The address, 5705 Luce Avenue, McClellan AFB, California, was soon etched in my heart. That White apartment manager never rented to any other people of color or minorities during our time there.

20 Eastbound, No Westbound

In 1964, I was on my second tour of duty. Gena was now four months old and the absolute love of our lives. My beautiful Maude had been engraved in my heart since the first day I met her and watching her as a mother made every day magical.

I had been trying to decide where to place a practice for some time. Washington, D.C. was attractive to explore as a permanent place to live. We believed the cultural and social conditions would be five-star compared to those in the South or mid-America. Maude encouraged me to fly back to D.C. to take the examination for licensure there. Upon completion, I was issued a license to practice in the District of Columbia.

Shortly after getting my license, I met a wonderful gentleman: a civilian dentist named Roscoe Brewer. He was a stalwart of the local Black community and one of its finest servants, promoting medicine and dentistry as careers for Blacks. Dr. Brewer was an exceptional human being, always helping others be successful. He was intelligent and forthright. To our family, he was a combination of advisor and father. I was a young dentist trying to decide what to do after separating from the air force and Dr. Brewer provided sacred, unselfish, and sound advice to help me make the best decision.

He described the advantages and disadvantages of life as a dentist, explaining some of the common obstacles that challenged Black dentists. To show his character and how sincere he was, Dr. Brewer offered to reopen his office for me during the evenings, even though he had retired and closed his practice. He did this for me out of the kindness of his heart. Because of him, I made the decision to become licensed in California. This gave me permission to practice in California, as well as in Washington with a regional license.

The California Board of Dental Examiners issued my license to practice dentistry in February of 1965. Dr. Brewer allowed me to practice dentistry a few evenings a week in his place. He encouraged me. It was now time for me to make the most important decision: to remain in California or return to the east coast.

My first year of this tour of duty was ending and the air force inquired if I would consider making a career as an Air Force dentist. They asked me to commit no later than early 1965, right when Gena would celebrate her first birthday.

Maude was now pregnant with our second child. Her mother, Rosalyn, traveled from North Carolina to California to assist Maude. We were elated that Gena would have a new baby brother—what a milestone! Brian was born in 1965. We thought perhaps the Spencer legacy of having large families was now in the making for the second generation. Rosalyn arrived shortly after Brian. Maude was happy to have her mom with her at this precious time and Rosalyn was a great help. She really enjoyed watching Gena, too, and comparing each of Gena's milestones with Maude's milestones when she was a baby—her first tooth, first time crawling, and every new word. We appreciated her being with us. The home-front was good, and our larger adopted entourage was happy for us.

On the work-front, the Vietnam War was in full bloom; many of my friends were engaged in combat and died during the war. Some were shot down on their first mission. The mission of our clinic was to prepare the airmen and pilots to engage the enemy in combat. The war was going on for nearly ten years and there was no end in sight. I had experienced enough deaths. I no longer wanted any part of that conflict, and no longer wanted to work for Colonel Fields. He still exhibited the same racist tendencies he had when I arrived at McClellan in November of 1963. I was honorably discharged in October of 1965.

Our family had a wonderful experience during that tour of duty after we moved onto the base. We were a little sad to leave. Maude loved the base and felt secure enough to leave our doors unlocked sometimes. Since she was pregnant during most of my two-year tour of duty, my wife, and our family, needed a vacation. Maude, Rosalyn, and the children flew—in order to avoid driving across country with two small kids—back east for rest and relaxation. I remained on the base to be processed out of the air force and base housing. Our furniture was placed in storage because we had not concluded whether to live on the west coast or the east coast.

We visited back east to predicate our final decision—D.C. or California. My cross-country drive was imminent. I made it to D.C. in less than three days, eager to see my family. After resting and visiting relatives for two days, I explored D.C. I consulted with classmates from the

Howard Dental School, the D.C. Dental Society, and the Medical Society to research locations as well as the market demand for dentistry. I found, in my market analysis, that supply and demand were key components of success in a free and capitalistic market.

I made a conscious effort to utilize my college expertise in economics as a basis for determining the best locale for a dental office. After a visit with relatives in North Carolina, I drove our family back to D.C. Again, we explored whether or not we wanted to live there to raise our family. I had experienced enough injustices and racial discrimination in North Carolina and Mississippi. We had already decided not to settle south of D.C. My contact with racial hatred and horrible treatment under Jim Crow in both Mississippi and the rest of the Confederacy had maimed my emotional state. I could not live among Whites in the South.

Maude and I thoroughly reviewed our options for raising our children in D.C. After consulting with other business owners and dental personnel, we decided, in a couple of days, to return to the Golden State. The first call I made was to Dr. Brewer. He welcomed us back to California with open arms. He ribbed me, saying he had known in his gut we would be returning soon. We packed the car and headed for California. It felt like we were two lunatic kids making a hasty getaway instead of sensible parents of two children. Arriving in Chicago for an overnight stay confirmed that we were westbound!

I was the lone driver while my wife tended to the babies. It was an adventure—part fantasy and part fairy tale. We were brave and daring and trusted we would arrive safely. Our air force friends, Bob and Bonnie Wright, welcomed us to Sacramento and sheltered us in their home. We stayed there for two weeks—with *two* babies! Bob was on active duty at McClellan. He had to report for duty at 7:00 a.m. after very little sleep, thanks to the nightly screams of our babies. Coincidently, a White air force sergeant transferring to Europe rented us his home in Rancho Cordova, just like the White sergeant who had rented us our first apartment two years earlier. Those two sergeants were ground-breakers who dared to close the racial divide to aid my family. We moved into our house at 2416 Palo Vista Way. In the midst of California redlining for the second time, we claimed our first home as civilians.

Because Dr. Brewer surmised I would return to practice in California, he had retained his closed office for me. He was the first Black health practitioner in Sacramento. He had opened his practice in, or around, 1932. He later encouraged Dr. Kenneth Johnson to join him in a group practice. Upon my return, in 1966, Dr. Brewer and Dr. Johnson planned and constructed a new medical/dental building at 1614 X Street in Sacramento. The building was considered to have a modern contemporary style and the dental office was occupied by Dr. Brewer and me.

Before the building was complete, I attempted to secure a loan from local banks to finance the purchase of dental equipment and other office products. I submitted loan applications to the Bank of California, Bank of Sacramento, Wells Fargo Bank, and Bank of America; all the banks refused to finance my practice, claiming I did not have any collateral for security. Yet all the White dentists from the air force who opened practices in Sacramento received loans immediately, without any collateral. Dr. Gary Newhouse, a close White friend, was very concerned that I was not approved for a loan. He even escorted me to the Bank of Sacramento on the very same day he was approved for a loan there, without collateral. The bank manager informed me a few days later that the loan had to be secured by collateral.

My credit was excellent; the banks refused my loan due to the color of my skin. They made loans to my White counterparts. Giving up on getting a loan was not in my blood. Daddy had tutored me to have faith during life's journey. With God's blessings, I attended an Omega Psi Phi fraternity meeting and met a brother from Morgan State University in Baltimore, Maryland named Tom Queen. Tom had been recruited by Bank of America to be an intern. I explained my dilemma to him and he agreed to check with his manager, Mr. Skinner. Tom was instrumental; I met with Mr. Skinner and explained that the banks refused to give me an unsecured loan.

On the same day he retired, Mr. Skinner proudly announced that, as a retirement gift to me, he was approving a loan in the amount of $9,000. I opened an office account with the bank branch at 9th and O. Mr. Skinner was a pillar that helped launch my dental practice. Maude and I were exhilarated and expected a happy future for our family.

We opened our practice and welcomed patients from Dr. Brewer's old office. Dr. Brewer was such a staunch supporter of our family and absolutely wanted me to be successful. He came into the office to greet his old patients and introduced them to me, as if he were passing on the torch.

Dr. Brewer, now Roscoe to me, had always been a special individual. He was unwavering in dignity, integrity, and uplift and he meant a lot to me. He had the vision and courage to aid me and others. Roscoe provided sound advice for a successful practice, including a few fundamental gems about patient-doctor relationships. He emphasized to never discuss politics, religion, or fees with patients. After years of experience, he asserted that these topics caused undue strain on any kind of relationship. He told me the dentist had to demonstrate professionalism at all times by remaining neutral and listening without passing opinions. Implementing these gems played a key role in developing my thriving practice.

A representative from the Bank of California came by my office unannounced, just after New Year's in 1966. He spoke with me about having my office account. After inviting him into my private office, I shared how his bank had refused my business a year earlier, and how his apology did not make up for his bank's previous actions. He subsequently understood that I was not interested in doing business with his bank, *period*! Other bank representatives came to my office seeking my business and likewise left empty-handed. I learned many things from Daddy, including his business acumen. He understood the value of any bank that would approve his loan, and the value of keeping that business relationship. I still value my relationship with Bank of America.

I continued to see Dr. Brewer's patients as I added new patients from the community. I was surprised when the non-commissioned officer in charge of the hospital cafeteria at McClellan walked into my office. He had heard from other airmen that I had opened the practice and came to say hello. I became his family dentist and our two families spent enjoyable time together.

21   Blessing One Blesses Others

Daddy continued to preach at multiple churches in Mississippi. He and Mother Dear continued to enjoy good profits from the farm business and shared their blessings within the community. My parents taught us to do our best always, to love without regard to skin color, to stand strong in our faith, and to believe in the power of God. Maude and I were blessed by so many relatives and friends once we married. Now Gena and Brian were toddlers, healthy and happy. My practice was quite rewarding, and our family had begun to enjoy its fruits.

Being a new African American dentist in town, a White dentist named Patrick Melarkey, introduced me to the local dental society and assisted me in securing and installing new office equipment. I attended the monthly dental society meetings cognizant that there was no socializing, or very modest contact, between White and Black dentists. The few Black dentists sat at a table alone during meetings. When Dr. Melarkey and Dr. Walt Griffin attended meetings, they were the only two White dentists who would sit with us. It was a brave move—they were courageous in welcoming me to Sacramento.

The Civil Rights Movement continued to be turbulent and unprecedented, led by Dr. Martin Luther King, Jr. during the 1960s. Dr. King expressed the principle of non-violence so eloquently on the steps of the Lincoln Mall during the March on Washington. He continued to fight for Black people to have the same social and economic opportunities and justice White people enjoyed. Myrlie Evers was also nonviolent in her work with the NAACP, even after the murder of her husband Medgar. Other non-violent groups, like CORE, held direct action campaigns opposing Jim Crow segregation and job discrimination, and fought for voting rights. This led some Blacks to organize the Deacons for Defense and Justice to eliminate violence by the KKK. According to Daddy, when this self-defense group was organized in 1964, violent struggles with the KKK in Mississippi and Alabama decreased.

President Kennedy called for the Civil Rights bill in the summer of 1963, but Republican congressmen took action to keep the bill bottled up in Congress indefinitely. Shortly after Kennedy's assassination in November of 1963, President Johnson told the legislators, "No memorial oration or eulogy could more eloquently honor President Kennedy's memory than the earliest possible passage of the Civil Rights bill for which he fought so long." The Civil Rights Act was signed into law by President Johnson on July 2, 1964.

In 1968, a group including myself, Dr. William Lee, Dr. Marion Woods, Dr. Howard Harris, Dr. George Stewart, and others established the Sacramento Urban League. Black unemployment was high, redlining was popular, and housing discrimination was prevalent. These injustices started by Whites were front and center in Sacramento and in America. We founded the Urban League to deter discrimination in housing and employment and to improve the treatment of Black people. Dr. Harris was the first executive director and I was the first president of the board of directors. Dr. Woods, Dr. Lee, Dr. Stewart, and others served on the board with great distinction; they were dedicated to the Sacramento Black community.

My sensitivity to discrimination in California, Mississippi, and the whole south compelled me to seek resolution through the Urban League. Amid discrimination against people of color, I attempted to purchase a home in South Land Park in the late 1960s. After several unsuccessful weeks, I was drained by so many "For Sale" signs and no opportunity to purchase a home. I was referred to Nat Colley, a distinguished and prominent civil rights attorney, who would help me buy a home. Mr. Colley assured me he had the appropriate agents to get through the rampant discrimination openly practiced by several realtors. The following week, Mrs. Schaber, a realtor (and mother of Gordon Schaber, the Dean of McGeorge School of Law), contacted me and arranged for Maude and me to revisit a home we had tried to buy. This time, the sellers accepted our offer and Mrs. Schaber closed the transaction. Though the process was painful, finally purchasing our first home was gratifying. We moved out of our rental and settled in without any issues, with gratitude and thanks to God.

The year 1966 included a glorious and crowning achievement for Daddy: he was chosen as president of the General Missionary Baptist State Convention of Mississippi. The mission of the Convention was to provide a state-wide organization for Black Baptist churches with which to promote Christian education, missions, discipleship, social services, ministries, and evangelism. Each president had his own vision;

the highlight of Daddy's vision was to eradicate racism and injustices suffered by his people.

Previously, when Daddy served as president of the Claiborne County Baptist Missionary Association, his mission was for Natchez College (founded earlier by the Convention) to provide schooling for Blacks beyond the level of education offered by Mississippi. Natchez College, a two-year school, provided education for poor Blacks, allowing them to receive higher education in southwest Mississippi. Most of their graduates went on to attend Alcorn Agricultural & Mechanical College on work scholarships. Daddy often stated, "No one can rob your knowledge, but they may rob your rights." Daddy carried this mission on to the General Missionary Baptist State Convention. He faithfully served as president with the strong conviction that good education was the solution for the advancement of Black people.

Dr. Martin Luther King, Jr. was assassinated on April 4, 1968. His death brought grief and heavy hearts for many, including Maude and me. Yes, I was speechless! I was overcome with sorrow and worried about the plight of my family and Blacks in America following his assassination. A dark period in race relations was cast upon this country. The whole world mourned his death. I was deeply hurt by that dastardly act.

Because they were powerless to express their discord, Black Americans nationwide reverted to rioting in many cities throughout the nation. Blacks destroyed wide areas by rioting, looting, and burning buildings in D.C., Los

Angeles, Detroit, Chicago, and other urban domains. Many citizens regretted those acts of destruction but understood that the social ills of discrimination caused the riots. Implicit in Dr. Kings' legacy was a blueprint for justice, peace, integrity, love, freedom, non-violence, and dignity. "Injustice anywhere is a threat to justice everywhere," as Dr. King so eloquently stated.

In the 1970s, I joined Dr. Melarkley in a group practice of ten dentists. We delivered comprehensive dental treatment. I owed allegiance to Dr. Melarkley and I was honored to be part of his assemblage. My relationship with him, both as a friend and as a dental colleague, was sincere and respectful.

Other organizations caught my attention in the '70s. Sacramento was ripe for Black leadership. I joined the board of directors of the Sacramento YMCA to project a goodwill image for Blacks. I also accepted membership in the NAACP to serve on its board of directors. While serving on the board, I convinced the other members to make the honorable Charles Evers (my old schoolmate and the first Black mayor of Fayette, Mississippi) a guest speaker at the annual fund-raising dinner. Mayor Evers delivered a historical message. He quoted the dreams and revelations of his brother Medgar and his struggles to obtain justice and freedom for Mississippi Blacks.

22 Where Did the Decade Go?

I continued my community involvement in the 1970s. I served on the Sacramento Library Foundation board of directors, which was thrilling. Since Maude was a librarian, I was even more excited for my appointment. I was also appointed Commissioner of the Sacramento City Housing Authority by the Sacramento City Council. Milton McGhee, Vice Mayor and another Black American, had nominated me for that post. McGhee solicited Mayor Richard Marriott for support and together they convinced the city council of the need for diversity. I was the first Black American to serve. In my first meeting, I was not accepted or welcomed in any congratulatory manner by the Chairman or any of my fellow commissioners; in fact, I was not even recognized. The meeting convened at a nightclub on 21st Street, in a private room owned by the Chairman, Robert Smith. After, I was not invited to join the group for post-meeting spirits. It was emphatically a good old White boy's network and they were undoubtedly racist in their deliberations.

Mary Irwin, a White commissioner appointed after me, extended her goodwill during the meetings and as others were appointed, our relationships became polite and respectful. Maude and I traveled to Oahu, Hawaii, to represent Sacramento in a national housing meeting. This meeting helped me understand the intricacies of public housing in America. I was elated to realize that redlining had been eliminated in federal housing for all people. The Housing Authority expanded construction of public and senior housing using federal money, thus making housing discrimination illegal and giving open access to all people of color. My nameplate was included with the other commissioners' names in the lobby of the buildings constructed by the Housing Authority. It was an honor.

In September of 1970, our third child, Arika, arrived and we could not have been happier. Gena and Brian were doing well in the Sacramento Country Day School. Having more children added more responsibilities, so I added hours in the dental office to increase my income. We were comfortable and well-established in Sacramento. We were happy with the decision to raise our family here and blessed to have huge support for my practice.

Our last child, Jennifer, was born in 1972. Her arrival blessed us: we now had two sets of children in the same age range. Jennifer was truly a good match for her big sister, Arika.

In some ways, history had repeated itself. My parents' goal, before I was even born, was to educate our entire family. They ingrained this dream in us by purchasing property near one of the Historically Black Colleges and Universities (HBCUs), and we all graduated from Alcorn Agricultural & Mechanical College.

More than 30 years later, on the opposite coast, Dr. Baxter Geeting had the same dream for his family. He met a math teacher from a small school and discussed his ideas for a school. By the fall of 1964, the school they envisioned was a reality. As an independent, co-educational, college preparatory school, the Sacramento

Country Day School was serving pre-kindergarten through the 12th grade. Enrolling Gena and Brian was a no-brainer for Maude and me; we wanted them to have the best education possible, even at that early level. It was an outstanding school, rated as one of the top elementary schools in Sacramento. Our family's legacy of education was now continuing in the second generation. I served on the board of directors of the Sacramento Country Day School. This motivated me to be active in the school's day-to-day operation.

I continued my work in the community to advance social and economic opportunities for all people of color. Black Greek letter organizations did not have a Sacramento Pan-Hellenic Council for communicating ideas. Marietta Scott and I founded one in the 1970s. I served as its first president; Marietta was its first secretary.

A series of visions for the community led me to assist in also organizing a state component of the National Dental Association. A few years later, the California chapter of the National Dental Association elected me to serve as its second president. The mission of the state chapter was to help Black dentists receive information and documentation on the latest treatment regimens. Very few Black dentists, if any, participated at the policy-making level in the California Dental Association during the 1960s and '70s. Therefore, very little information trickled down to lone Black American dentists. In fact, we gained more information from the dental supply companies than from the state association. The local Black dentists (Dr. George Stewart, Dr. James Martin, Dr. Kenneth Ponder and I) shared information often by simply picking up the telephone.

Once again, we organized: we created a Sacramento chapter within the state chapter of the National Dental Association. The Black dentists voted for me to serve as the first president. With support from the dentists, we were able to unite with the local Capital Medical Society Chapter (an affiliate of the National Medical Association representing Black physicians). With our combined efforts, we raised funds for academic scholarships. Thanks to these scholarships, young Black students gained more opportunities to achieve higher goals. We dentists spanned out within our communities, sitting on more and more boards to ensure that the level of information and effort met our requirements.

Mother Dear and Daddy came to California to visit my family. Maude and I watched as they cherished each grandchild, showering them with hugs and kisses, just as Big Mama had done to me and my siblings. My parents had so much love and admiration for my children, and my children returned their love and affection. By now, Daddy had received his Doctor of Divinity, an advanced academic degree in divinity. Through meditation and dedication to his ministry, he had the Holy Spirit of God within him. He and Mother Dear connected with Maude and me in a spiritual way that was full of familial passion and devotion.

Both my parents exercised their thoughts and Christian beliefs by caring, comforting, and consoling the entire family. This led to our ultimate bond as one unit of gratification. Daddy's spiritual meditation spilled over during his visit and seemed to be the core of his religious convictions. Because I inherited my parents' desires to fill the cup of the Holy Spirit, I sought a place of worship for us. On a bright Sunday morning we all huddled in our vehicle and headed off to a church whose pastor, Reverend Jones (a retired army colonel/chaplain), was one of my patients. The church service was more than wonderful. Reverend Jones shared that he and Daddy had met before at the National Baptist Convention as allied Baptists.

Reverend Dr. Eugene Spencer, Sr. delivered a spiritual sermon to the congregation. Our family was thrilled watching Daddy participate in the service with his eyes and body language so clearly at ease in the house of the Lord. I believed he was overjoyed within. Mother Dear and Daddy's noticeable spiritual conscience was recharged on that day as they worshipped surrounded by their grandchildren. After a wonderful, heartfelt two-week visit, they departed for Mississippi.

I was a bit taken aback that they chose to return to Mississippi, a state with Jim-Crow venom dripping from its seams and indescribable hatred toward Blacks. On a positive note, my parents were seldom confronted by Whites. I attempted to determine why they were not confronted more in their later years. Although they lived in a segregated society still fueled by racism and Jim Crow, they kept to themselves and avoided encounters with Whites. Also, as self-employed business owners through farming and their ministry, they did not depend on Whites for financial support.

In the 1970s, Daddy recommended I purchase approximately 2,000 acres of timberland on the Mississippi River. The property had a dock on the river for barges to transport the timber north and south in the country. He called and advised me that profits from the timber alone would pay off the loan. An arrangement with the Port Gibson bank secured the loan. My signature was the only requirement left for the purchase. I decided to let that opportunity pass. It was a colossal business mistake. Another owner, a White man, did make the purchase and he paid off the loan a few years later. During this time, Daddy served as the first Black president of the Claiborne County Farmer's Co-op, which was a milestone during the Jim Crow era. He reminded me often that I would have been a millionaire "over and over." He was correct—that business venture became the pillar of income for Claiborne County.

In 1975, farming was still attractive to me. I had a lengthy conversation with Daddy about the likelihood of using some of his land devoted to agricultural farming. Since he was not growing crops anymore, we agreed that starting a cattle farm would be an adventure and worthwhile economically. However, Daddy was miffed I wanted to engage in undertaking a farm plan that required concerted efforts and time for success. I recognized that Daddy was really slowing down physically. He suggested I employ someone to assist in managing the herd daily and I did. Initially, I purchased about 15 cattle, along with the necessary facilities for feeding and maintaining the herd. Although it was a wonderful experience and quite rewarding, I decided to end my cattle farming at the end of the third year.

From 1973 to 1977, it was my honor to serve again as president of the Sacramento Urban League's board of directors. Through the efforts of the executive director, Delores Bryant, several members, including me, became members for life. The Urban League's primary mission was to reduce unemployment for Blacks and establish equal opportunities and justice within the criminal and civil court system. During my presidency, our board was baffled when Ronald Reagan, then Governor of California, accepted our invitation to speak at the Urban League's Black History Program. That was our largest fund-raising effort during my tenure; several corporations made substantial contributions. To our surprise, Governor Reagan gave an interesting speech on race relations, discrimination, and solutions. The next Governor of California, Jerry Brown, refused our invitation to speak at the Black History Program, due to scheduling conflicts. Sources indicated that Governor Brown did not believe in special programs sponsored by the Urban League.

Discrimination and racism toward in-state and out-of-state dental applicants were rampant in the Board of Dental Examiners, not only against Blacks, but also Asian Americans, Jewish Americans, and any other minorities. Governor Brown appointed a Blue-Ribbon Committee to investigate the board's discrimination. The committee included the four Deans from the University of California San Francisco (UCSF), University of California Los Angeles (UCLA), University of Southern California (USC), and

Loma Linda University. Dr. Henry Lucas and I, both Black dentists, were also chosen by the Governor to serve.

For two days, in San Francisco, the six of us were mandated to review records and make recommendations to the office of the Governor. We observed blatant patterns of bigotry and discrimination by the Board of Dental Examiners. For example, the board documented some of the applicants with identifiers like "Jap," "Negro," "China," "Jewish," "out-of-state," and other designations. Photos of all applicants were required and there was a concerted effort to push forward candidates from only California dental schools. Our major recommendations were to eliminate all photos and racial identifications on application forms and to promote diversity of the examiners—previous examiners were all White male dentists from California schools who colluded before issuing grades for each applicant.

The Governor's office accepted these recommendations and others. A diverse board, appointed by Governor Brown, made changes to institute the new guidelines. Black dentists were appointed to the board and I volunteered to be an examiner for the licensure examinations. Because of the changes, more ethnic dentists entered the profession. Shirley Jordan (a colleague, schoolmate, and fellow Howard grad) became the first Black female president of the California Board of Dental Examiners.

While serving as president of the Urban League, I had lunch with Joseph Cooper, JD, my predecessor. We decided to form a California Legislative Committee for the local Urban League to gain political clout with the state legislature. Joe and I believed that because we had Black elected officials serving on key legislative committees, the Urban League could play an adversarial role at the state level to influence legislation. Joe agreed to draft the initial by-laws for this committee and a presentation for our board. The by-laws were adopted, and the local Urban League sponsored a state-wide meeting at the El Rancho hotel in West Sacramento.

Representatives from Urban Leagues throughout California attended along with the NAACP, both state and local politicians, and representatives from the Governor's office. Joe and I presided over the meeting. Out of that gathering, the Black American Political Action Committee (BAPAC) was formed. The Black politicians and political staff became very active and used the organization as a means for political gain. The anticipated mission of the Urban League was undermined by Black politicians and staff and was used by some as a tool for Black political advancement in California. Percy Pinckney, from Governor Brown's office, for example, influenced Willie Brown and other Black politicians to be active in the organization. He eventually used this as a focal point to promote Black legislative ideas. Certainly, I was proud that the BAPAC was being used to advance the cause of Black elections and legislative processes.

The 1970s were filled with enthusiasm. I became one of the founders of a local chapter of Omega Psi Phi. The other members elected me its first president. Our membership immediately became involved in Sacramento's civic activities.

The members appeared before authorities governing the California State University system to help Dr. James G. Bond, the first Black president of CSUS (from 1972–1978), continue his presidency. We were successful—Dr. Bond was able to serve out his remaining term. The Omegas formed an alliance with the Urban League and the NAACP to eliminate segregation and racism in Sacramento.

Some of the notable Omega Psi Phi members included Marion Woods, PhD (founder of the Sacramento Urban League); Willie Ellison, PhD; Colonel George S. Roberts (famed Tuskegee Airman); Carleton Adams, MD; Ervin Jackson, PhD; Wilson Riles (CA State Superintendent of Education); Reginald Young; Thomas Slaughter, MD; James Martin, DDS; Seymour Daniel; Excetral Caldwell; Randolph Cooke, JD; Leander Roberts; John Braxton; and Luther Nolan, EdD.

By the end of the 1970s, Gena and Brian had graduated from Sacramento Country Day School and were enrolled in high school—Gena at St. Francis High School and Brian at Jesuit High School. Arika and Jennifer were attending St. Michael's Episcopal Day School, an outstanding private elementary school.

23   A Decade of Change

In the early 1980s, Dr. Charles Townsel, president of the Urban League Board, consulted with me about organizing a statewide association of black educators. However, because I was not an educator, I felt awkward about participating in such a venture. Dr. Townsel suggested the Urban League take the leading role in formulating this organization. He believed the educators would be sympathetic to the possibility of joining with the Urban League. As a member of the board, I was finally convinced to explore the merits of starting that alliance. I had many questions about how this would aid Black children in the classroom. Would this organization be a beacon of hope for more Black students, encouraging them to attend college? Would test scores, including the SAT and ACT, improve in urban schools for impoverished children? Would school districts encourage our best teachers, with pay incentives, to teach in these neighborhoods?

The local Urban League Board, along with Dr. Townsel, invited leading Black educators from across the state to a planning session. Out of this meeting, the California Alliance of Black School Educators was formed. The first convention was held in Sacramento in 1982. I was surprised at this convention when the Alliance presented me with the Distinguished Service Award, which read, "IN RECOGNITION OF YOUR INSPIRING AND CONTINUED DEDICATION IN HELPING TO IMPROVE THE QUALITY OF LIFE OF BLACK PEOPLE." This indeed was the culmination of my participation, outside the dental profession, to achieve the advancement of my people.

Also in the early '80s, I was introduced to an Ethiopian student, Daniel Amare, who was enrolled in graduate school studying chemistry. He became my dental patient. As I treated him, I became closely acquainted with his academics and encouraged him in his educational endeavors. After a series of dental treatments, he asked me to sponsor members of his immediate family, so they could come to America. After some thought, I advised him that I would have to check with immigration authorities before undertaking such a vast responsibility. As usual, I also discussed this with Maude, whose motherly instinct, I knew, would be helpful in evaluating such an undertaking.

With four children, I was hesitant to assume that sponsorship. It was a guaranteed financial obligation for the well-being of those young students. Since they were from Ethiopia, I felt I had a moral responsibility to assist them in achieving an education. Finally, I decided to file the appropriate papers to sponsor Daniel's sister, Martha Amare. She came to America with the understanding that I was her financial caregiver. We agreed she would live with Daniel and I would provide her with a dental assistant job in my office. This assured Martha the funds she needed for survival in the U.S.

Martha immediately enrolled in Sacramento City College. She graduated with honors, then enrolled in the engineering school at CSUS. During the school year, Maude and I decided to sponsor another brother, Zachariah Amare, because Martha had performed so well scholastically. The immigration authorities readily approved his entry into the country, perhaps because of Martha's academic accomplishments. Later, he graduated from CSUS with a degree in architecture. We sponsored yet another brother, Thaddeus Amare, who completed his undergraduate requirements at the University of California Davis (UCD). Thaddeus continued his education in medical school and earned his medical degree.

The children's mother, from Addis Ababa, visited our family. She brought gifts of appreciation and spent a long evening with us, thanking us and expressing her gratitude. She even invited us to visit Ethiopia.

Eventually, Martha enrolled at the University of Washington and graduated with honors. I encouraged her to attend dental school and she matriculated in the School of Dentistry at UCSF. Martha graduated and opened her dental practice in the Bay Area. I am extremely proud of these young Ethiopians who exhibited hard work in their endeavors.

I continued my efforts to assist others obtain their licenses to practice dentistry in California. Four dentists from the Philippines interned in my private dental office in preparation for their California dental licensure exams. We had lengthy discussions as I reviewed theory and practical examinations (lab) and their formats. All four dentists were licensed to practice dentistry in California. This was the crown jewel of my efforts to aid others in my profession. Over the span of years in my practice, Black dentists were given the opportunity for employment upon graduation or completion of their residencies. It was incumbent upon me to give back. I remembered how Dr. Roscoe Brewer played a key role in assisting me and supporting me at the beginning of my practice. I still truly admire and appreciate Roscoe's thoughtfulness.

While I supported others, I envisioned my own life's ambition, but it was interrupted by Daddy's untimely death in 1983. I experienced a weary load of unknown expectations. It seemed impossible for me, during this ordeal, to focus on or continue on without Daddy's erstwhile advice and conversation. My inner thoughts and perceptions stood still in a pattern of behavior that was unbelievable. I wondered how life would be without him. When I returned home for preparation of his final services, conversations with Mother Dear and my siblings eased my pain.

Daddy was a giant among humankind and a father of fathers to his family. He was sincerely concerned about the injustices toward Blacks, particularly the impulsive, Jim Crow practices committed by Whites in Mississippi. Now that he was gone, the world seemed to float on endlessly. My closest mentor was no longer physically present, but his vision, love, and wisdom carved out a foundation for me to rest upon. He had provided scholarly advice about society, politics, and business throughout my entire life's journey. He was also simply my father. Well done, Daddy. Sleep in peace. The uncompromising character who laid the foundation for my travels, I still miss him.

Maude's parents had already transitioned. Her father, Herman Walters, died in 1967 and her mother, Rosalyn Walters, died in 1971. Their passing caused both of us heartfelt sadness. I was sure this presented a challenge to Maude; she had to stabilize her young children while comforting her siblings and relatives during that period of sadness.

The year 1983 brought mixed feelings of fellowship as social values, shared interests, and attitudes blossomed into more Black history groups. I was still grieving Daddy's death. A young Black lawyer, Gary Ransom (currently a retired superior court judge), shared his idea of beginning a local Boulé of the Sigma Pi Phi Fraternity—a group of noble, educated, and distinguished Black men with like goals and values. I had multiple memberships in other Black organizations, was raising four children with my lovely wife, and had biased opinions about assembling another group. Gary was sincere and direct in his deliberations. He was insistent about founding this noble group of Black men.

He suggested he and I convene a meeting at my dental office for further discussion. During our meeting, Gary proposed that I host the first group meeting at my home. After a lengthy talk, I convinced Gary I had to get my wife's approval to host. During our second meeting at my dental office, I agreed to host the first group meeting at my home. He had a strong will and after several conversations, I knew "no" was not the appropriate answer. In the following months, I hosted a meeting of seven Black men — six physicians and one California State Supreme Court Justice. Among the group of seven men, to my surprise, was John Norton, MD, a schoolmate and friend at Howard University. John, presented

a compelling presentation to organize a Boulé.
Quite naturally, I was more than influenced after
his detailed lecture about the organization.

These men, along with a group of other
local, accomplished men, sponsored the
organizing of the local Boulé. The Boulé was
founded in 1984. Its members included dentists,
physicians, lawyers, educators, and an architect.
The Boulé was a vibrant component of the Black
experience, sponsoring impoverished Black high
school students to attend HBCUs and sponsoring
social programs for high school basketball. In the
same year, with two dental practices, I prepared
to limit my work to be near home and my family.
I closed my downtown Sacramento office in 1984
and concentrated on transferring my patients to
the other office in the Country Club Medical
Plaza. This was more convenient because it was
closer to home. My practice's population had
grown tremendously; as a result, I added two
associates to accommodate the patient load. I
decided to reduce my days in the office. Thanks
to God, it was a success.

The experience I gained as a board member
of the CSUS Trust Foundation was truly
awesome. Being directly exposed to different
management structures and strategies—including
fund-raising techniques—reinforced my vision
for a better community. The board was composed
of community volunteers. We brainstormed,
dreamt, and translated our ideas into some
philanthropic enterprises. I benefited from this
task immensely—two of my children graduated
from CSUS and Maude received her master's
degree in media communications there. I was
destined to give back to the University for the

opportunities it afforded my family. Gena graduated from UC Davis in 1986 and Brian graduated from UC Berkeley later. Both Arika and Jennifer graduated from El Camino Fundamental High School (a gifted program designated by the San Juan Unified School District) in 1988 and 1990, respectively.

In December of 1989, I was inducted into the Hall of Fame of the *Sacramento Observer*, the African American newspaper. The *Observer* proclaimed, "Dr. Eugene Spencer has long been a leader in the dental profession. In fact, he served a term as president of the influential California Chapter of the National Dental Association. Dr. Spencer's leadership in dentistry is well-deserved. He has worked hard developing a successful practice over the last three decades, gaining the respect of his patients, his fellow professionals and the community. It only seems like yesterday (in the early '60s) when Dr. Spencer was providing free dental care to low-income Black youth who could not afford such services. He has demonstrated his leadership in his community too, with the devoting of his time, energy and resources to many organizations and causes. For five years, for example, Dr. Spencer served as chairman of the board for the Sacramento Urban League. A recent Gallup Poll revealed that dentistry is the second most respected profession in America. With leaders like Dr. Spencer, it's understandable why. We are proud to salute him as one of our first business Laureates."

Mother Dear, my rock, transitioned in 1989. Her death was just as untimely for me as Daddy's. We never want our loved ones to go, even though we know it is a natural part of life. It was sad and very stressful for our family. I was left to shoulder the burden in the aftermath.

Mother Dear's advice was profound and lifted my life's journey. She was the bulwark of our family and laid the foundation for the success of our clan. On numerous occasions, she protected her children from the dangers of society. I experienced it firsthand as a youngster in Mississippi when she would not allow me to hang out with "thugs" or, as she often said, "people of unpleasant character."

She was adamant about her children not going to nightclubs and associating with people drinking alcohol. I remembered way back when I wanted to go to that nightclub. She said, "You are not going." I replied, "Mother Dear, you think I am better than my friends." She came up close to me, glared at me straight in the eye, and said, "You *are* better than those so-called friends." That left a lasting impression on me. I cherished her and shared her advice with my own children. Mother Dear's love and passion for her children and family were unquestionably ingrained in all of us. I love you, Mom.

24 We Need a Vacation

Maude and I were adventurous enough to spend a few weeks in Europe. We splurged on each other and traveled to London, Amsterdam, Cologne, Heidelberg, Munich, Innsbruck, Florence, Rome, Venice, Pisa, Zurich, and Paris. We landed first in London—the gateway to Europe—and were startled by the sheer size of Heathrow Airport. The massive crowds of travelers were pummeling each other. We were surprised by so many wonderful restaurants, cafés, and bars, and we had fun sampling quite a few delicious foods. We were excited to visit Harrods Luxury Department Store in Knightsbridge, London. We satisfied our curiosity about the costs of luxury designer fashion accessories. The tour of the store was exciting, and the product services were exemplary.

We took a thrilling voyage by hovercraft over the North Sea to Holland. We saw the fabulous windmills and art galleries. The windmills were an engineering feat—pumping water from the lowlands back into the rivers. We watched a Dutch woman carve a pair of wooden shoes from virgin wood. First, she used an axe to roughly shape the shoe from the water-saturated poplar wood, Next, she used a lock knife to skillfully shape the shoe. Finally, she turned the spoon drill and carved out the inside of the shoe, shaving away little by little until the vision in her heart matched the object in front of her. Once they were carved, they were hand-painted in beautiful bright colors. It took hours to complete a single pair. That ancient art was full of suspense.

Our arrival in Amsterdam was filled with mystery. On warm nights, beautiful girls were displayed in the Red-Light District for carnal gratification. Our canal cruise was simply picturesque. Beautiful romantic lights illuminated the scenery. On a previous vacation, we took a tour of the diamond mines in West Africa. They were owned by a Dutch company; West Africans received no financial rewards from their country's own diamonds. We enjoyed visiting the art galleries in Amsterdam, Venice, Rome, and Paris. While we adored all the galleries, Amsterdam's art galleries were more intriguing in their creativity and contemporary art.

The BMW factory in Munich, Germany caught my eye. I was impressed with how immaculate the premise was; all the employees wore matching white coats and helmets and the floors were spotless. The cars were pristine and flawless. The parts on the production lines and the various machines in the factory could have easily been in a contemporary art gallery. Our BMW visit reinforced my love for German cars, with their classic designs and engineering. Touring the *autobahn*, a super-expressway designed for high speed traffic and lacking speed limitations, appeased my desire to experience sleek sport cars. Porsche, Ferrari, and Lamborghini cars gleamed down the expressway. When my German friend, an economic minister, shipped a Ferrari via air from Munich to Los Angeles, my interest in sports cars increased tenfold. It was a crowning moment when I drove that red beauty to Sacramento. Wow!! I was in another world.

Michelangelo's sculpture of David in Florence, Italy, exhibits the male anatomy in its finest concept. David, the masterpiece of the Biblical hero, is a 17-foot marble statue of a standing male nude. It is an art favorite in Florence. For our next adventure, we visited the Vatican's Sistine Chapel in St. Peters Basilica and saw the ceiling painted by Michelangelo. Of the artist's many works, the ceiling is a striking masterpiece. We visited the Vatican and it was breathtaking. At the Vatican, my biggest surprise was the size of the Sistine Chapel. For some reason, I expected a colossal structure covering a block or two, but it was not that large. We visited world famous clothing designers' offices and factories, including the finest in leather goods in Rome. The Colosseum was our last destination in Rome. It was an intriguing structure from the Roman Empire that still stands. The Amphitheatre was completed in 80 A.D. and was used for gladiatorial contests and public spectacles.

We went on to Pisa where we observed the Leaning Tower, built in the 12th century. I was startled to see that the Tower is still standing considering the angle of tilt, and how it gradually increased until the engineers completed the calculations to stabilize the structure. Venice, the city on lagoons with buildings that "seem to be swimming or floating on water," presented an aura of mystery about the architecture and engineering used in construction of its buildings. A scent or odor, maybe from fish or marine life invading or sharing the surrounding environment, emanated profusely as we toured the various attractions around the city.

The tour guide advised us to look offshore to see the island of Malta. I am not sure my vision clearly allowed me to view the coastline. According to our guide, Churchill, Roosevelt, and Stalin made plans to defeat Nazi Germany on Malta. There were also postwar European plans made on the island in 1945 (known as the Yalta Conference). We were most appreciative to find our way to Switzerland because the finest meals we ate were in Lucerne. We sojourned in the watch factories and jewelry stores, attempting to make purchases at reduced cost—with no luck, of course. Our visit to Zurich was enlightening. It was quite surprising to learn that Zurich, founded by the Romans, became the center of the Protestant Reformation in Europe. I was interested in the Swiss watch companies and curious about the banking system.

We liked Zurich and the Swiss food, however, our tour to the Swiss Alps presented a breath of "pure" air—literally. At times, near the peaks, it felt like I was out in space wondering if I would be able to return to civilization. It was quite frightening.

Paris was our last destination before departing for the USA. It is really a world class city of art, fine dining, international flare, the Eiffel Tower, and many interesting sites. Paris is known for its leading role during the Age of Enlightenment. It was also one of the first European cities to adopt gas street-lighting. It was a fitting end to a wonderful trip to be in "The City of Light." I was there with the love of my life who is also the light in my life. Bonjour to the French citizens!!

Our Europe trip made me take a walk down memory lane. I thought about our trip to West Africa, our homeland, in the late 1980s. We flew from New York's Kennedy Airport to Senegal on an overnight flight. The flight was full of Senegalese going home. They carried the most unusual packages of goods destined for their countrymen and relatives. Our complete culture shock began as our flight ascended. The passengers forced their belongings into every available space, which was sometimes on top of another passenger's belongings. We arrived in Dakar to connect with our tour. Our flight connecting with the tour in New York arrived late from San Francisco.

After checking into the hotel, we immediately joined the tour and went to Goree Island, the departure point of the Atlantic slave trade. We observed relics of the chains and equipment used to conquer the slaves for the Atlantic voyage. Maude and I had an eerie sensation when we stood in the huts made for holding the slaves before the ships went out to sea. We were sad and almost tearful from the experience, knowing that our ancestors probably came from that area. The tour to The Gambia included a visit to Juffure Island. The show *Roots* was filmed there with LeVar Burton starring as a slave named Kunta Kinte. We were acquainted with LeVar, who is a native of Sacramento, and his family. Alex Haley, who wrote the book *Roots*, attended the Alcorn Prep High School and Alcorn Agricultural & Mechanical College before his 20-year career in the United States Coast Guard.

We continued on to Ghana, where we toured the W.E.B. Dubois Memorial Center in

Accra. Dubois and his wife are buried there. Our tour carried us to the gold mines in Ghana. Most of the mines were owned by Dutch companies and the manual labor was done by the natives. The gold was shipped to Holland for processing and worldwide distribution. Many of the African countries that we toured remained poor due to corrupt politicians who were always being paid off.

Our itinerary included a stop at the main holding site for the Atlantic slave trade. We entered a dungeon-like building. The elevated master's quarters provided a view of the women in captivity, waiting to be sent out to sea. Our tour guide told us that the master often selected a female for sexual gratification who was then taken upstairs to his quarters. The slaves occupied the holding tanks for several days, or even months, before being loaded on the ships bound for the west. Within the holding tank, an area was marked off to illustrate that while the slaves waited to be sent across the Atlantic Ocean, calcified human waste accumulated 18-inches deep.

We next visited the Ivory Coast. The French had influence throughout the Ivory Coast. French contemporary architecture appeared all over the city with wide landscaped Boulévards leading into the capital, Abidjan. Poverty was prevalent among the population, even though the country was the world's largest grower of cocoa beans. Probably the most remarkable site we toured in the Ivory Coast was the largest Catholic Church in the world, the Basilica of Our Lady of Peace. It was completed in 1990 as a gift from President Felix Houphouet-Boigny, the first president of the

Ivory Coast. According to the priest there, thousands of peasants attended services weekly, mostly impoverished and uneducated, though the church was constructed with expensive gems, gold, murals, and other riches. The President's palace is massive and surrounded by a moat with crocodiles in it for security.

Upon completing our West Africa Tour, we left Dakar and returned to the U.S., enriched with African art and the lovely African culture and mores. We were blessed on both trips.

25 Good Deeds Produce Good Returns

The 1990s continued to bless our family. Arika received her bachelor's degree from CSUS in 1992 and Jennifer received her bachelor's degree from CSUS in 1994. This was the conclusion of the second generation of our family legacy of education. Maude and I were so proud of our children, and we knew that all our parents were dancing in heaven over their accomplishments.

In 1995, we went off to North Africa. Egypt beckoned us. We decided to explore Egyptology in a class setting. Dr. Asa Hilliard, an African American Egyptologist, invited us to join him on an excursion entitled "The Royal Holy Family," sponsored by the Ancient African Heritage Study Tour. We arrived in Cairo to begin our study tour and were bewildered by the traffic congestion. Donkeys, camels, wagons, and automobiles co-mingled. The first day, we visited the Cairo Museum and saw the mummified bodies embalmed by Egyptians so many years ago. We also viewed the King Tut exhibit. In Cairo, hearing the sounds of the call to prayer from the mosques was a daily ritual and it became part of our daily expectations. We decided to attend a service to gain knowledge about their religious protocol.

On our third day, we ventured out to the great pyramids—architectural wonders three times over. To this day, many marvel at how man could have built such a wonder. I decided to enter the largest pyramid, the Great Pyramid of Giza, and ascend to the top. I quickly discovered that there was no elevator nor stairs to walk up. One could only crawl up the stairway. The succeeding steps were maybe 4 to 5 inches higher than the preceding steps and constructed, I believe, in stone. After a few minutes of ascending through a narrow passage, it became horrifyingly dark. I suddenly made the decision to not continue to reach the first chamber of the pyramid; my instincts led me to start descending rapidly, subconsciously. My retreat seemed unending, although it was probably ten minutes or less before I reached the exterior and saw Maude touring around the base of the pyramid. It was a happy reunion indeed, to be with Maude and the outside world again.

We visited the Great Sphinx with anticipation, believing it would be massive in size. It was truly monumental. The nose was defaced, and it is alleged by some historians that Napoleon, during the French campaign, shot the nose off. Yet, according to our instructor, Dr. Hilliard, there was no concrete evidence that Napoleon or any other despot did that. The camel ride was short and dusty, and the temperature was extremely high. Both of us were eager to return to the hotel and arrange our trip to Memphis the next morning.

Our excursion to Memphis was like a step back into Egypt's history. Memphis was the ancient capital of Aneb-Hetch, located just south of Giza. Dr. Hilliard provided lengthy Egyptology lectures about the region. We learned that "Kemet" was the ancient Egyptian name for "Egypt." According to the lectures, many people forget that Egypt is part of the African continent and only think of Egypt as a modern state with ties to the Islamic world.

Luxor was our next stop. We digested the historical information introduced to us by Dr. Hilliard. The next day, we were happy with our overnight stay on Banana Island on the Nile River. It was close to nature and eco-friendly. The Aswan Dam on the Nile River, which forms Lake Nasser and supplies water to Egypt and the Sudan, is a wonder and a feat of classical engineering. Tourists from all over the world were visiting the Aswan Dam and a large contingent of Japanese citizens were photographing the site.

Our two weeks of study ended in Abu Simbel in Nubia, near the Sudanese border. Our graduation concluded with a libation—a ritual of heritage in African culture—on a waterfall. Upon boarding the airplane for our return to Cairo, Dr. Hilliard's assistant got into a heated confrontation with the airplane crew. This was daunting for Maude and me. We prayed we would be able to fly back to Cairo. During the encounter, suddenly army troops occupied the airplane with AK-47s. We wondered if they were going to escort our entourage to prison. The crew on the plane and some members of our group were involved in the fray, hurling epithets. Maude quickly aided in diffusing the situation by kindly asking the members of our group to "Please be quiet and take your seats." After about an hour of war-like action on the plane, a soldier de-escalated the conflict and we departed (thank God).

My perspective of civilization, and of my own African heritage, was enriched immensely from my trip. It was good to get back home and back into our normal routines. My practice was growing, and Maude was still enjoying working in the main library.

My alumni institution nominated me for an honor for making significant contributions to American Society: "Dr. Eugene Spencer, Jr. is one of the outstanding graduates of historically black colleges and universities (HBCUs) being honored as Distinguished Alumni at National Association for Equal Opportunity's (NAFEO) 21st National Conference on Blacks in Higher Education." Later in the year, I was nominated by Alcorn (now "Alcorn State University") for the Presidential Citation, awarded by the National Association for Equal Opportunity in Higher Education. This award recognized exemplary experiences that honored my alma mater. I flew to Washington, D.C. to accept that honor. I was also inducted into the Alcorn State University Hall of Honor that same year.

The following year, I was devastated with the news that my dear sister, Rosia, had transitioned. I had always known that Rosia was the smartest, by far, of my siblings. Maude and I made plans to travel back to Mississippi for her funeral. It was good to see her son, Harlan, and his family, although I wished it were under different circumstances.

In December of 1998, the *Sacramento Observer*, in celebration of its 35th anniversary, submitted a list of 35 "Legends" — the most significant and influential African Americans in the city's history. The *Observer* saluted me as one of their legends. The *Observer* stated, "Dr. Eugene

Spencer is more than a successful dentist. He is a respected community leader. Over the past three and one-half decades, he has served on many of Sacramento's most important and prestigious boards and foundations, devoting time, energy and resources to causes important to the development of the community. Born in Port Gibson, Mississippi, Dr. Spencer is a graduate of Howard University Dental School. From his first arrival in Sacramento, Dr. Spencer has shared his talents and profession with city residents. Never forgetting his roots, Dr. Spencer served for many years as president of the board of the Sacramento Urban League and a board member of the Sacramento Branch NAACP. He is a former commissioner of the Sacramento City Housing and Redevelopment Agency and a board member of the CSUS Foundation. A strong family man, Dr. Spencer has always been a proponent of providing greater opportunities for today's youth. He has demonstrated his commitment by helping to open the doors of success for many who have followed him."

For Black History Month, in 1999, the Greater Sacramento Urban League extended honors to me for exemplary service to the African American community as a leader, mentor, nurturer, and healer. The plaque was special because I was a co-founder and the first president of the Urban League Board many years ago. I was impassioned about receiving that honor.

On June 18, 1999, two white-supremacists set fire in the Country Club Medical Building including my dental office. Maude and I had arrived in Boston the day before the fire. Our plans were to vacation on Martha's Vineyard for two weeks. A vacation of love and relaxation inspired our thoughts of a get-a-way, only for the two of us. A midnight call from Brian, my son, detailed the damage to my office. We returned the next day to assess the damage; the city fire inspectors advised us to close the office. After a few weeks, construction of my office was initiated and completed in a timely manner. I was a bit frustrated because I was not sure if I was a target or not. The investigation revealed that an abortion clinic in the building was the main target. In my mind, it was difficult for me to conclude that my office was not a target because of the excessive damage. I may have been sensitized by past racial injustices experienced. These Jim Crow experiences will remain with African Americans in the pursuit of justice.

I continued my post-doctoral education at the UCSF School of Dentistry; the UCSD School of Medicine; and the University of the Pacific School of Dentistry. As a practicing dentist, my goal was to provide patients with high ethical standards of care and excellent treatment. I was happy that I put forth my best efforts in delivering care. My practice was a model of diversity: the patient population was probably 75% Caucasian, 15% African American, and 10% other. I regretted that African Americans did not seek dental treatment in a timely manner, as compared to Whites. They were also mostly unamenable to preventive care. Premature tooth loss and poor oral health are common for African Americans and economics undoubtedly play a role in that.

My greatest joy occurred when I treated the Olympians Bill Russell, Wilma Rudolph, Ruthie

Bolton, and Evelyn Ashford. All of them won gold medals in their disciplines. Russell was unassuming and very quiet in my office, as was Wilma Rudolph. Wilma's magic and personality were special. She was very loving and hospitable, exuding congeniality. She was also seemingly preoccupied. Evelyn was friendly, yet very serious about life. She was positive toward mankind, cordial and obliging. Ruthie, full of joy with a bubbling personality, was willing to help "everyone." She was quite spiritual, loving, and big-hearted. These Olympians were unique in character and left a lasting impression on my life as their dentist and friend. Their affable ethos brought friendship to humanity. May God bless them.

In 2003, Alcorn State University, in commemoration of the 50th Anniversary of the Class of 1953, presented the Golden Diploma to me with sincere appreciation and admiration.

My brother, Harold, transitioned in 2005. He had spent his entire Army tour of duty in New Mexico and then returned to Claiborne County for a position at Alcorn in the business office. He married, started his family, and made Claiborne County his home. Maude and I traveled back home for his funeral.

The years seemed to fly by much faster in those days. I continued to serve the community in any way I could, making it possible for young African Americans to enter the dental or medical fields. In 2008, the United College Action Network (U-CAN) saluted me, as one of their prestigious honorees, for my dedication and commitment to the organization during its 20th

Anniversary celebration. U-CAN sponsored high school students to enter HBCUs.

My dedication to mankind was revitalized when Barack Obama was elected as the first African American president in 2008. His election made history and African Americans were in awe, highlighting their race with pride and great delight. Maude and I journeyed back to snow-covered D.C. for his epic inauguration in January of 2009. We found peace in the cold, freezing weather—one would have thought we were preparing for an exploration in Antarctica.

We were thrilled to attend that historical inauguration. According to the media, there were 1.8 million Americans in attendance, along with news media from around the globe. Our Hilton hotel was just across the Potomac in Arlington, Virginia. Since we lived in D.C. before, I had anticipated throngs of people riding the rapid transit going to the inauguration. As expected, when the trains approached our station, they were fully packed with passengers. After a long wait, we decided to board the train going in the opposite direction and then board again at the initial station. The inauguration was a memorable and historical event that will remain in our hearts forever.

In 2010, I decided to retire. Although none of my own children chose to pursue a dental career, Gena's husband, Glenn Middleton, chose to purchase the practice. It was a great relief. I rejoiced when Glenn decided to assume the practice and carry on the family tradition. Just as Roscoe had done for me so many years ago, I introduced my patients to Glenn, addressed all of their concerns, and made sure they understood that they were in good hands.

Later that year, I lost my youngest brother, Delano, three months before his birthday. He had been suffering from cancer. I knew he was finally out of pain and in the arms of Mother Dear, Daddy, Rosia, and Harold. Each of them guided me during my life's journey. Now, Doris and I are the last remaining survivors of our family.

26 Life after Retirement and Other Random Facts

Maude and I celebrated 51 years of marriage in 2014, resulting in a reaffirmation of our blessings, love, and respect for each other. We decided to sojourn to Martha's Vineyard. The Vineyard attracted our attention because of its proximity to Cape Cod and our admiration of President Kennedy and the Kennedy Compound. President Obama and his family also chose Martha's Vineyard as a vacation haven.

Dr. Arnold Graham, a dental classmate, had a home on the Vineyard. We shared time together, recalling our dental school experiences and the final week before graduation. The Grahams prepared a celebratory dinner for us that Maude and I really enjoyed. We were indebted to them for their hospitality.

We explored the Oak Bluffs of the island, an area steeped in African American History. Oak Bluffs represents upward mobility for African Americans. African American slaves settled on the island in the late 1800s. When they became free, they constructed charming cottages. Charles Shearer, the son of a slave, opened the first cottage for African Americans. Over the years, many charming cottages have been constructed to create colorful structures beaming off the Atlantic Ocean. Oak Bluffs is a getaway for the African American élite.

We toured Edgartown, Vineyard Haven, and Aquinnah, which is known for its beautiful clay cliffs and quiet natural serenity. The island is a paradise and offered freedom for African

Americans. The African American Heritage Trail tour is a celebration of life for African Americans and other early island settlers. The tour's legacy is to celebrate their values (like justice), their love, and their pride for all of their accomplishments around the island—including having their own homes. It was a monumental task for those trailblazers and the tour is an honorable tribute.

In 2015, I received the Captain Award from the Alcorn State University Alumni Foundation for financial contributions. The staff and student population are diverse at Alcorn State University, with students from around the world and from multiple ethic groups—Whites, too. That shift was a monumental metamorphosis of profound significance. Back when I attended, an African American male would have been arrested if he had a relationship with a White female. Likewise, if an African American female had a relationship with a White male. During a visit to my alma mater, it was remarkable for me to observe the staff and students in such close harmony. It was a great gift of happiness, and it felt like some of the old Jim Crow was fading into the past.

In September of 2015, with U-CAN's assistance, 25 students from Sacramento were enrolled at Alcorn State University. I chose to spend some of my retirement time assisting U-CAN in recruiting students for my alma mater and other HBCUs. I believe education is a highway for African Americans to escape from poverty and to experience less injustice and discrimination in our country.

The Sacramento Urban League observed their 50th anniversary in April of 2018. That historical moment was etched in the lives of the few living founders who envisioned the goals of abolishing discrimination and seeking justice and employment for African Americans in the community. Dr. Marion Woods, Dr. William Lee, and I are the only living founders of the Sacramento Urban League that I know of. According to sources, Dr. William Lee is confined to his home with health concerns. I pray for God's blessings to strengthen and guide him daily. Dr. Howard Harris, a founder and the first executive director, recently transitioned.

I continued giving back to mankind by agreeing to serve on an advisory board in conjunction with Alcorn State University and UCD. The board collaborated with African countries to assist in farm production and agribusiness. My degree in agricultural economics attracted my interest. The collaboration provided me with an opportunity to increase my knowledge of modern agribusiness. Observing farm products being made start to finish reminded me of my early childhood in Mississippi.

A considerable amount of my retirement time is dedicated to African American youth. Currently, I am spending some time each month recruiting students for Alcorn State University and Howard University. According to U-CAN, approximately 100+ students currently attend Alcorn State University, and more will be entering in September of 2018. Retention of students is the key focus of the pilot program. The program develops support plans that enhance students' abilities to return to college each new school year. Immediate academic, psychological, and social supervision plays a major role in retention. In the 2014–2015 school year, the retention rate was 92% and students embraced college life quite well. Our objective is to help African Americans reach élite status in science, technology, engineering, and mathematics, and to produce future leaders for America and the world. As my parents stated, "A college education is an escape from poverty for African Americans and, to some degree, an escape from injustices spawned by American society."

In November of 2016, Donald Trump was declared President-Elect of the United States of America. I was perplexed, horrified, and bewildered by his statements against the democratic candidate, Hillary Clinton, during his campaign. I saw that Donald Trump is xenophobic, sexist, misogynist, and racist, and I saw how he mocked a disabled journalist. I questioned whether he was fit to serve as President. The country is divided along racial lines with racism ingrained into the ilk of our society. My children and other young people are very concerned about their future in this country with Donald Trump as President. I pray for my children.

Brian, my son, has been diligent and stayed the course for several years, aiding and recruiting low-income African-American students for college. I commend him for his dedication and forthrightness in getting his mission accomplished. Brian graduated from UC Berkeley and chose to exert his influence by recruiting for HBCUs. It is a mystery to me how he is so exceptional at encouraging even honor students to seek an HBCU education. My daughter, Gena, who graduated from UC Davis, has also begun to recruit students for Alcorn State. Maybe recruiting for HBCUs is how they have chosen to carry their education-legacy forward. The fact that they were able to actually witness how the professors and greater community nurture Alcorn students probably played a key role in their loyalty to their mission.

On September 6, 2017, Hurricane Irma severely damaged the beautiful island countries of Sint Maarten and Saint Martin in the Caribbean. Maude and I experienced the most enjoyable and wonderful vacation of our lives there. The people were extremely warm and caring toward us when we were tourists. We were saddened for the gracious people on both sides of the island, Dutch and French, and we prayed for them. I sorely regret the devastation of the world-famous Princess Juliana International Airport. I will always remember seeing the beach-goers at Maho Beach as our plane ascended on our way home.

Our travel excursions led us to visit Hilo, Hawaii to explore opening a dental office there. Edward Briscoe, MD, a classmate and friend from Howard University, was practicing medicine on the island. We explored the idea of opening a comprehensive health clinic to cover different medical specialties. We toured the volcanoes that spilled lava over large areas of the island. Along with our two youngest children, Maude and I visited Hilo Bay and Rainbow Falls. We enjoyed the aura of the natural island experience. When the week was over, we concluded that we should do more research after returning home. A few months passed, and Dr. Briscoe decided to move to St. Thomas in the Virgin Islands.

Earlier, Maude and I had cruised to the Caribbean. Our ports of call included Haiti, Santo Domingo, the Virgin Islands, Puerto Rico, Fort Lauderdale, and Miami. We enjoyed the night-life in San Juan and the shopping in St. Thomas. In fact, we almost missed our departure from St. Thomas because of Maude's shopping spree. I think we were the last to board the ship!!!

27 My Wish

I was blessed to have wonderful parents who had a vision for themselves and for the family they would create together—"Education, education, education." Even before I could formulate what these words meant, I knew I was gifted into a special family. I was the first experience my father had as a Daddy. I watched him turn the Word of God into the living Word of experience. He believed in God and believed what He said and did. Through his actions, Daddy chose to share his love of God with everyone who crossed his path.

I am the first child Mother Dear gave birth to. She was a living example of her name—the dearest, most nurturing, loving, kind, gentle, and strong mother. When I think of her, I'm told my eyes sparkle and my dimples appear, as if I were still a child. She invoked warmth, trust, and a feeling of safety. With her I was truly "familiar"—closely intimate and well-acquainted. It was quite thrilling to watch Mother Dear and my youngest sibling graduate together. Mother Dear became a teacher at the Port Gibson elementary school for Negroes and taught there for many years. Her gratitude, love, and caring will always be an inspiration and a reminder of the keen vision God gifted her. I wish she was here to enjoy these kind words of true admiration and endearment. I love you Mom!

I started working before I started school. I learned that my narrow corner of the world was not fair to anyone with my skin color. There were laws to keep me from stepping outside my boundaries, and many lost their lives just being in

213

the wrong place at the wrong time. Our parents taught my siblings and me, by example, to always stay together, work together, and want the best for each other. With their guidance, our family legacy continues to be handed down from generation to generation and handed out in concentric circles through mentoring and sponsorship.

I could not—no, *would not*—be who I am, or have accomplished what I have, without my beloved wife, Maude. She is the love of my life, my beautiful gift, my partner for more than half of my life. Every new day with her is the best day of my life. I am truly grateful that she has been willing to share this journey with me. She is the "Mother Dear" to our children and grandchildren. Each of our children and grandchildren are brilliant and blessings for us. We have always taken time to live and learn together; work and play together; travel together; and pay our blessings forward, with hope that they will continue to do the same.

Sports have been an integral part of our lives. The outpouring of energy from sports provides relief from our daily regimens. We have had season tickets for the Sacramento Kings since 1985—the year the team first came to Sacramento. We also had season tickets for the Oakland Raiders for many years. Those games were our fun weekend excursions. We attended the Oakland Raiders/Minnesota Vikings Super Bowl in Pasadena, California in 1977. We have attended the Golden State Warriors' games. My heart is full at a sporting event and my energy level is off the scale. When my children were school-aged, we went to high school basketball and football games. It was a big celebration—like a party.

Our family's educational heritage is carried on by Gena, our oldest child, who is pursuing a doctorate in Asian medicine. She has traveled to Japan several times, completing continuing education courses in her beloved profession. She is scheduled to receive her degree later this year. As a teenager, Gena served as a consultant to the Sacramento County Juvenile Justice Commission. According to a commissioner, the commission adopted some concepts presented by Gena. The commission was able to streamline conditions related to the incarcerations of juveniles.

The adventures continue into the third generation. Our two grandsons, Harrison Eugene Brown and Brian Alejandro Spencer, are straight-A students, continuing the family legacy of education. I am beaming with pride for all of their achievements as young African American males. Brian, with aspirations of being a commercial airline pilot, is taking lessons on the simulator at the former McClellan Air Force Base. According to him, "I flew to London, England, landing without a problem, and then flew on to Paris, France." (He did not have a return flight on his itinerary.)

Harrison was presented with an MVP trophy in basketball by the Amateur Athletic Union (AAU) in the Bay Area recently. He plays point guard and has indicated that dentistry may interest him. Harrison and Brian enrolled in the academic summer school program for young kids at UC Berkeley. Students from around the world attend these sessions and the international exposure and culture have enriched their lives immensely.

There is one person I don't know much about and have thought of often throughout the years—my father's mother, Rose. Daddy never spoke of her. I have often wondered about her, not knowing her deeds, or if Daddy looked like her, or whether he learned to work so hard from watching *her* work so hard. I wondered if Daddy conversed with his brother about her. I inquired about her once and Daddy chose not to elaborate or discuss anything related to her. Mother Dear did not speak of her either and kindly advised me: "No discussion."

Distant relatives alleged that she traveled from plantation to plantation in Mississippi accompanying a White master's demand for fornication. During this period, Rose was impregnated by the White master and had her two sons—my father and his brother. She transitioned suddenly at 32 and relatives believed her death was caused by the jealous master. Daddy, at a young age, was reared by his uncle. It is understandable why Daddy would not talk about her. White masters infiltrated the African American family structure and having children out of wedlock became the norm. I attempted to trace my ancestry to my grandfather and beyond but was unsuccessful because records were not deemed important for African Americans in Mississippi.

I believe the appellation, or designated name, Spencer originated from my father's step-father or a White master. There is no documented evidence of this, however a friend uncovered a link that may provide some clues. In an online genealogy record of Daddy's profile, there are a couple of names listed under "Father" and the race is listed as Caucasian. Sadly, I never knew Rose and she is not listed in my father's online profile. Even though Daddy never spoke of Rose, he chose Rosia's name because it was close to his mother's. If my children or grandchildren want to know more about my grandmother, Rose Spencer, I will do all I can to help them.

Finally, I have recently learned that my father was written about in a book by Emilye Crosby entitled *A Little Taste of Freedom: The Black Freedom Struggle in Claiborne County, Mississippi* (Chapel Hill: University of North Carolina Press, 2005). The author notes, "As the number of sharecroppers declined, African Americans now worked at the box factory or as day laborers and domestics. Joined by an increasing number of African Americans in the aspiring class, those with some economic independence, *Reverend Eugene Spencer* worked with whites to try to improve African American schools."

The legacy continues.

About the Author

Eugene Spencer, Jr., is a social justice activist who has spent the better part of his life devoted to advancing equal opportunities for all African Americans. He holds a Doctor of Dental Surgery (DDS) from Howard University. He completed Post Doctoral Study at the University of California San Diego (UCSD) School of Medicine, UCSF School of Dentistry, and the University of the Pacific (UOP) School of Dentistry. When the pathways for such opportunities were unequal or unavailable, Eugene engaged the necessary resources to create whatever was needed.

Eugene is originally from Claiborne County, Mississippi, and grew up on a farm picking cotton, soy beans, melons, greens, and other vegetables. Eugene learned the agribusiness from his father who acquired his own property, built three homes, and hired many field hands as seasonal workers to become one of the most successful African American businesses of its time.

That business fueled the educational aspirations for the entire family. Eugene was the first to enter college, studied agricultural economics, and graduated with honors.

After relocating to the Sacramento Region, and establishing his dental practice here, Eugene sat on the Board of Directors for the YMCA, the Sacramento Library Foundation, California State University, and others. Eugene and his distinguished colleagues became founding members of the Sacramento Urban League.

Eugene is a co-founder and was the first President of the Sacramento chapter of the National Pan Hellenic Council. Eugene and Joe Cooper, JD were co-founders of the Black American Political Action Committee (BAPAC) under the auspices of the Sacramento Urban League.

Eugene continued to promote African-American studies at Alcorn State University, above and beyond, through his philanthropic contributions.

Eugene currently lives in Gold River, CA. He can be reached at esjrdds1@sbcglobal.net.

Appendix

The following pages contain photos of family, the property where I grew up and various accolades I received throughout my career.

"Big Mama"
(Mary Jane [Watts] Young)

"Mother Dear & Dad"
(Reverend Eugene Spencer, Sr. and Pauline Spencer)

Reverend Eugene Spencer, Sr.

Eugene's parents and siblings
(Delano, Rosia, Harold, Doris
Eugene - upper right corner)

Dad, Mother and Family Friend repairing lawn mower

Eugene's Baptismal Ceremony with children in the creek

Eugene's mom and dad with Rosia's son Harland

Family group photo at Mercy Seat Missionary Baptist
Church

Mercy Seat Missionary Baptist Church

Highway leading to the family property

Forestry on the family property
(both pictures)

Front of the family home built by Reverend Spencer

Backside of family home

Barn on family property

Eugene in the Air Force
First Tour of Duty

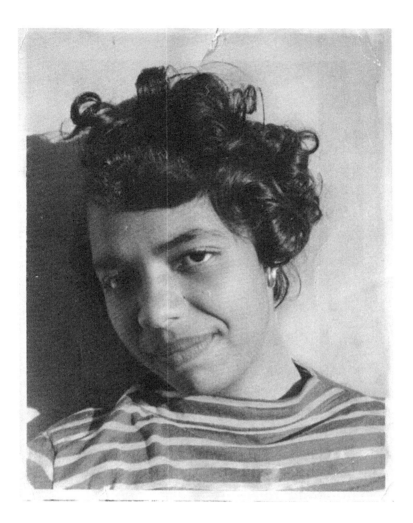

Maude in college

Eugene and Maude's Wedding Reception

Maude

Maude and Eugene

Maude and children - Daughter-in-Law - Janet, Gena, Arika, and Jennifer

Children - Jennifer, Gena, Arika, and Brian

Grandchildren – Brian and Harrison

Eugene with Harrison and Brian

Maude and Eugene

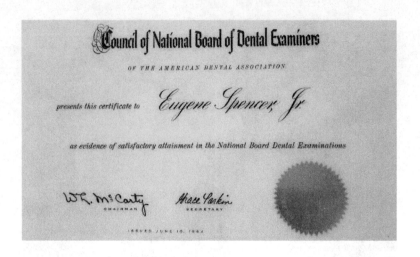

Graduation certificate from Dental School in Latin

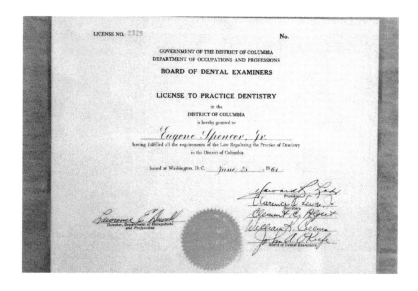

LICENSE NO. 2329   No.

GOVERNMENT OF THE DISTRICT OF COLUMBIA
DEPARTMENT OF OCCUPATIONS AND PROFESSIONS

BOARD OF DENTAL EXAMINERS

LICENSE TO PRACTICE DENTISTRY

in the
DISTRICT OF COLUMBIA
is hereby granted to

Eugene Spencer, Jr.

having fulfilled all the requirements of the Law Regulating the Practice of Dentistry
in the District of Columbia

Issued at Washington, D.C. _____ *June 25* _____ 19 61

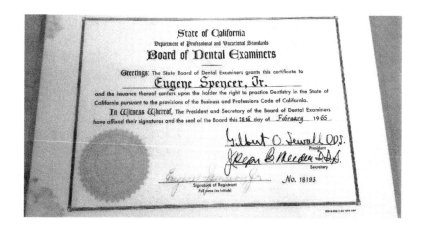

State of California
Department of Professional and Vocational Standards
Board of Dental Examiners

Greetings: The State Board of Dental Examiners grants this certificate to

Eugene Spencer, Jr.

and the issuance thereof confers upon the holder the right to practice Dentistry in the State of
California pursuant to the provisions of the Business and Professions Code of California.

In Witness Whereof, The President and Secretary of the Board of Dental Examiners
have affixed their signatures and the seal of the Board this 18th day of *February* 19 65.

No. 18193

241

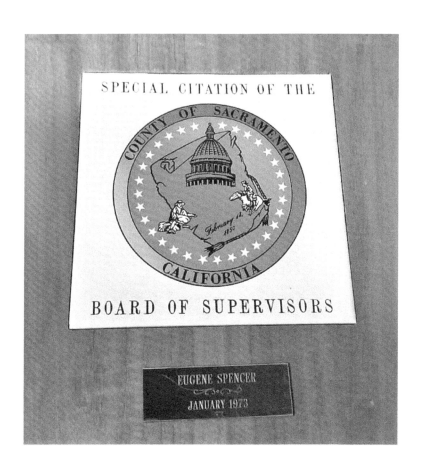

SPECIAL CITATION OF THE

COUNTY OF SACRAMENTO
February 14, 1850
CALIFORNIA

BOARD OF SUPERVISORS

EUGENE SPENCER
JANUARY 1973

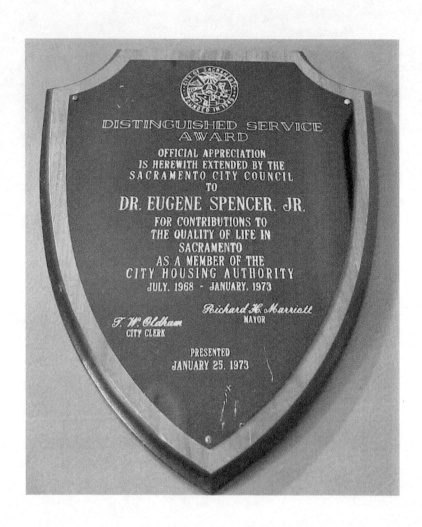

Presidential Citation

To

Eugene Spencer, Jr., D.D.S.

In recognition of exemplary
experiences that honor your

Alma Mater

one of the historically black institutions
awarded by the

National Association for Equal Opportunity in Higher Education

Witness: _____

Chairman of the Board, NAFEO

_____

President, NAFEO

Saturday, April 20, 1996

At Washington, District of Columbia

Resolution

JUNE 17, 1974

WHEREAS, Dr. Eugene Spencer, D.D.S. has served capably and well as a Commissioner of the Sacramento Housing Commission since July, 1968, and

WHEREAS, during that time, Dr. Eugene Spencer, has held the office of Vice Chairperson of the Housing Commission, from 1970 to 1971, and

WHEREAS, the Sacramento Housing Commission recognizes the merit of the service as well as the time and effort expended by Dr. Eugene Spencer during his six years tenure,

NOW, THEREFORE, BE IT RESOLVED BY THE SACRAMENTO HOUSING COMMISSION, that Dr. Eugene Spencer, D.D.S. is hereby officially commended for his past ministrations as a public servant and fellow Commissioner.

MARY M. IRWIN, *Chairperson*

ROBERT TRUJILLO, *Vice Chairperson*

ACHILLE R. ALBOUZE

MARIAN R. LOZANO

LESLEY L. LUEVANO

WILLIAM S. SELINE, *Secretary*

Mentor - Dr. Brewer
First African American Healthcare Practitioner in Sacramento, CA

Eugene Spencer

DISTINGUISHED SERVICE AWARD
Official appreciation is herewith extended
by the
SACRAMENTO CITY COUNCIL
to
EUGENE SPENCER, Jr. D·D·S
Member,
CITY HOUSING AUTHORITY
SACRAMENTO HOUSING COMMISSION
July, 1968   June, 1974
Vice—Chairman 1970—71

Jaci H. DeFord
CITY CLERK
Richard H. Marriott
MAYOR

Presented June 20, 1974

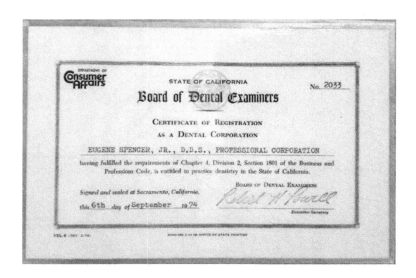

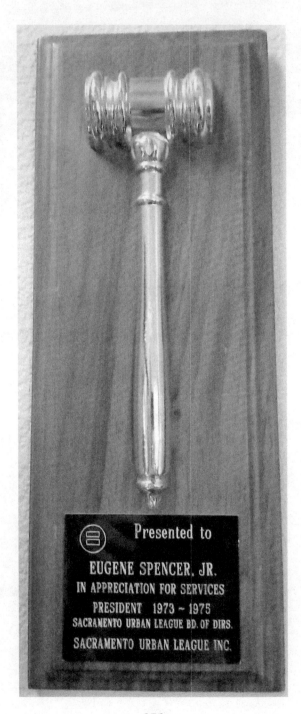

Presented to

EUGENE SPENCER, JR.
IN APPRECIATION FOR SERVICES
PRESIDENT 1973 ~ 1975
SACRAMENTO URBAN LEAGUE BD. OF DIRS.

SACRAMENTO URBAN LEAGUE INC.

250

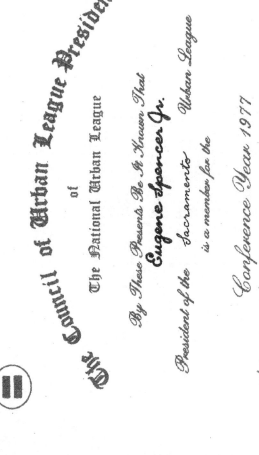

The Council of Urban League Presidents
of
The National Urban League

By These Presents Be It Known That
Eugene Spencer Jr.
President of the Sacramento Urban League
is a member for the

Conference Year 1977

251

SACRAMENTO PAN HELLENIC COUNCIL OFFICERS

OUT GOING

IN COMMING

PRESIDENT:
JACK PAPIN
KAPPA ALPHA PSI

PRESIDENT:
ALVA YOUNG
ZETA PHI BETA

VICE PRESIDENT:
CHARLES FORD

VICE PRESIDENT:
CLEVELAND HAMPTON

RECORDING SECRETARY:
ALVA YOUNG

RECORDING SECRETARY:
GALEN S. ROBINSON

TREASURE:
WINDIE SCOTT

TREASURER:
ELNOR TILLSON

PARLIAMENTARIAN:

PARLIAMENTARIAN:
NATE HUNTER

MOTTO: COMBINING EFFORTS FOR COMMUNITY DEVELOPMENT.

HONOREES

EUGENE SPENCER, Jr.D.D.S
Founder & First President
1978 - 1980

JEANETTE HAMPTON
President
1980 - 1982

JACK PAPIN
President
1982-1985

The National Pan Hellenic Council was founded at Howard
University in 1930. Charter members were: Alpha Kappa Alpha
Delta Sigma Theta, and Zeta Phi Beta Sororities, Kappa Alpha
Psi and Omega Psi Phi Fraternities. Alpha Phi Alpha and
Phi Beta Sigma joined in 1931.

PRESIDENTS AWARD
In Recognition Of
EUGENE SPENCER, DDS

For Your Outstanding
Service To The Community
MAY 1993

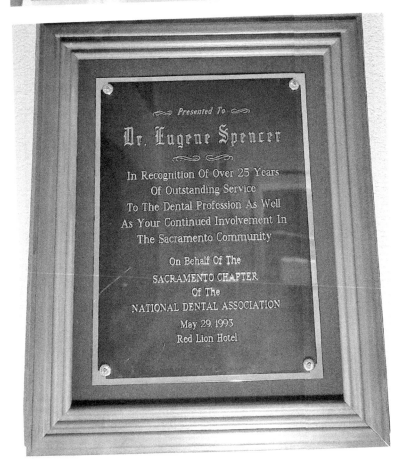

Achievement Award
For Outstanding Community Service
Dr. Eugene Spencer

Epsilon Xi Chapter
Omega Psi Phi Fraternity, Inc.
May 29, 1993

Presented To
Dr. Eugene Spencer

In Recognition Of Over 25 Years
Of Outstanding Service
To The Dental Profession As Well
As Your Continued Involvement In
The Sacramento Community

On Behalf Of The
SACRAMENTO CHAPTER
Of The
NATIONAL DENTAL ASSOCIATION
May 29, 1993
Red Lion Hotel

Resolution

By the Honorable Diane E. Watson, 28th Senatorial District;
Relative to Commending

Eugene Spencer, Jr., D.D.S.

WHEREAS, Dr. Eugene Spencer, Jr., was recently honored by the Sacramento Chapter of the National Dental Association for his many years of outstanding professional and community service; and

WHEREAS, A native of Port Gipson, Mississippi, Dr. Spencer graduated from Alcorn State University Laboratory High School and went on to earn a Bachelor of Science degree in agricultural economics from Alcorn State University; and

WHEREAS, After pursuing graduate studies at the University of Maryland and the American University in Washington, D.C., he received a Doctor of Dental Surgery degree from the Howard University School of Dentistry in Washington, D.C. in 1963; and

WHEREAS, From 1963 to 1965, Dr. Spencer was a captain in the United States Air Force Dental Corps; and

WHEREAS, In 1965 he began his private dental practice, with Dr. Brewer in Sacramento, and since that time, he has continued in his private practice; and

WHEREAS, Highly respected in his profession, Dr. Spencer has been a member of the American Dental Association, the California Dental Association, the Sacramento District Dental Society, the Sacramento and California Chapters of the National Dental Association, and the California Board of Dental Examiners; and

WHEREAS, He served as an appointee of Governor Jerry Brown on a special committee to investigate discriminatory practices by the California Board of Dental Examiners; and

WHEREAS, Dr. Spencer is a founder and past President of the Sacramento Sigma Pi Phi fraternity, the Sacramento Chapter of Omega Psi Phi fraternity, and the Sacramento Pan Hellenic Council; and

WHEREAS, Committed to enhancing the quality of life of his community, he has been active in the Sacramento Housing Authority, the Sacramento Urban League, the Sacramento NAACP, the Sacramento YMCA, Sacramento Country Day School, the Sacramento Library Foundation, California State University, and the Sacramento Trust Foundation; and

WHEREAS, He receives the love and support of his wife, Maude, and his four children, Gena, Brian, Arika, and Jennifer; and

WHEREAS, Not content to pursue his highly successful career, Dr. Spencer has given extensively of himself to help meet the needs of his community, and his spirit of dedication has served as an inspiration for all who aspire to professional excellence; now, therefore, be it

RESOLVED BY SENATOR DIANE E. WATSON, That she takes great pleasure in commending Dr. Eugene Spencer, Jr. for his exemplary display of responsible and dedicated service to his profession and community, applauds his many accomplishments, and conveys best wishes for every success in the future.

Member Resolution No. 618.
Dated this 7th day of July, 1993.

Diane E. Watson

Honorable Diane E. Watson
28th Senatorial District

STATE OF CALIFORNIA

SENATE
RULES COMMITTEE

RESOLUTION

By President pro Tempore of the Senate David Roberti;
RELATIVE TO COMMENDING

Dr. Eugene Spencer, Jr.

WHEREAS, The Sacramento Chapter of the National Dental Association is sponsoring "An Evening of Appreciation" on May 29, 1993, at which time Dr. Eugene Spencer, Jr., will be honored for his many years of dedicated professional service and for the vital role that he has played in improving the quality of life in the local community; and

WHEREAS, Dr. Spencer was born in Port Gibson, Mississippi, and after graduating from Alcorn State University Laboratory High School, he went on to receive a Bachelor of Science degree in agricultural economics from Alcorn State University in Mississippi; and

WHEREAS, He pursued graduated studies at the University of Maryland and the American University in Washington, D.C., and he earned his Doctor of Dental Surgery degree from the Howard University College of Dentistry in Washington, D.C.; and

WHEREAS, Dr. Spencer served as a captain in the United States Air Force Dental Corps from 1963 until 1965, when he opened his own private dental practice in Sacramento, where he has continued to practice since that time; and

WHEREAS, He has been affiliated with the American Dental Association, California Dental Association, Sacramento District Dental Society, Sacramento and California Chapters of the National Dental Association, and the California Board of Dental Examiners; and

WHEREAS, Dr. Spencer was appointed by Governor Jerry Brown to a special committee to investigate discriminatory practices by the California Board of Dental Examiners; and

WHEREAS, He is a founder of the Sacramento Sigma Pi Phi fraternity, the Sacramento Chapter of Omega Psi Phi fraternity, and the Sacramento Pan Hellenic Council; and

WHEREAS, Long active in his community, Dr. Spencer has been affiliated with the Sacramento Housing Authority, Sacramento Urban League, Sacramento NAACP, Sacramento YMCA, Sacramento Country Day School, Sacramento Library Foundation, and the California State University-Sacramento Trust Foundation; and

WHEREAS, He and his wife, Maude, are the parents of four children, Gena, Brian, Arika, and Jennifer; and

WHEREAS, Dr. Spencer has contributed extensively of his efforts to help meet the needs of the community, and he has earned the great respect and sincere friendship of all who have had the pleasure of associating with him; now, therefore, be it

RESOLVED BY THE SENATE RULES COMMITTEE, That Dr. Eugene Spencer, Jr., be honored for the significant contributions that he has made to his profession and to the people of the local community and throughout the state, and extended sincere best wishes for continued success and happiness in the future.

Senate Rules Committee Resolution No. 315 adopted May 24, 1993.

David Roberti

CHAIRMAN
SENATOR - 20TH DISTRICT

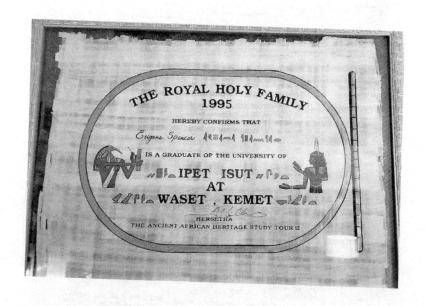

Congratulations

DR. EUGENE SPENCER, JR.

on your induction
into the

Alcorn State University
Hall of Honor

MAY 11, 1996

GREATER SACRAMENTO URBAN LEAGUE

Honors

Dr. Eugene Spencer Jr

For Exemplary Service to the African American Community as a
Leader, Mentor, Nurturer, and Healer

1999 BLACK HISTORY MONTH

James Shelby, President and CEO

February 26, 1999

Alcorn State University

Alcorn State   Mississippi

Be It Known that in Commemoration of the Fiftieth Anniversary of the Class of 1953

This Golden Diploma is Presented to

Eugene Spencer, Jr.

With Our Sincere Appreciation and Admiration

Given at Alcorn State, Mississippi, May 10, 2003

President of the University

Director of Alumni Affairs

263

United College Action Network

Salutes

Dr. Eugene Spencer

for your continued dedication and commitment to our organization and to the students that we serve. We are proud to name you as one of our prestigious honorees at our Twentieth Anniversary Celebration.
We look forward to your future support.
Presented the eleventh day of September, Two-Thousand Eight.

Dr. Alan Rowe
Founder and President

U-CAN

Donna Rowe
Founder and Chief Administrator Officer

Special

Appreciation

Award of Recognition for

Dr. Eugene Spencer

and his outstanding Leadership on the

Restroom Project Team

Cordova Baptist Church

2009

Pastor Ronald S.Johnson

Grand Boulé
of the
Sigma Pi Phi Fraternity

Resolution on the Occasion of Celebrating the 30th Year Anniversary

of

Gamma Epsilon Boule, Sacramento, California

Whereas, the Grand Boulé of Sigma Pi Phi Fraternity recognizes that Gamma Epsilon Boulé was chartered on July 7, 1984 in Sacramento, California; and

Whereas, Gamma Epsilon Boulé has sought the society of one another, both for the mutual benefit and to be an example of the higher type of manhood; and

Whereas, on July 7, 2014, Gamma Epsilon Boulé celebrated 30 years of commitment to the betterment of its community through social action activities; and

Whereas, the following Archons were charter members of Gamma Epsilon Boulé:

Willie A. Bell	Louis J. Johnson	Eugene Spencer, Jr.
John M. Carson	Raymond J. LaSure	John L. Spencer
Randolph Cooke	James D. Martin, Jr.	Eugene D. Stevenson, Sr.
John W. Hudson	Gary E. Ransom	Alfred Travis

Be It Resolved, that the Grand Boulé of Sigma Pi Phi Fraternity does hereby commend and congratulate Gamma Epsilon Boulé for 30 years of distinguished and honorary service and commends Gamma Epsilon Boulé for upholding the virtues of Sigma Pi Phi Fraternity and all that it represents.

Be It Further Resolved, that Gamma Epsilon Boulé receive a copy of this Resolution, expressing gratitude for this member boulé and appropriately honoring the Archons and Archousai for their outstanding service to the Fraternity and the Community in which they serve.

Be It Finally Resolved, that a copy of this Resolution be filed amongst the permanent archives of Sigma Pi Phi Fraternity.

In Witness Whereof, We hereunto subscribe our names and affix the seal of the Grand Boulé of Sigma Pi Phi Fraternity this thirty-first day of August in the Year of Our Lord, two thousand and fourteen.

James O. Cole, Grand Sire Archon

Samuel W. Bacote III, Grand Grammateus / Grand Secretary

ALCORN STATE
UNIVERSITY
ALUMNI FOUNDATION

CAPTAIN AWARD

Dr. Eugene Spencer

For Your Financial Contribution to
Alcorn State University
February 27, 2015
Dr. John E. Walls, Jr., Chairman

July 11, 2016

Dr. Eugene Spencer
11625 Gold Country Blvd
Gold River, California 95670

Dear Dr. Spencer:

As we embark upon a new academic year, I am happy to express my sincere appreciation to you for all of the work that you have done to assist in helping students to matriculate here at Alcorn State University. I know that you take great pride in being an alumnus of Alcorn State University. This is eminently obvious in your conversations and in your actions. Your advocacy for your alma mater, particularly for students in California, is commendable. Indeed, you serve as a great role model for all alumni.

There are many challenges which confront us in these times. Federal and state legislation and policies have tremendously effected how we operate. Federal financial aid policy changes in recent years have challenged the very core of our mission. Yet, we are committed to providing opportunities for young men and women who might otherwise not have a chance to pursue a college degree.

In spite of our challenges, I am optimistic about the future. We will continue to provide access to a quality education to a diverse population and we will expand our recruiting efforts all across this nation. With your help, we will be successful. Thanks for all that you do to support Alcorn State University.

Respectfully,

Alfred Rankins, Jr.
President

Office of the President | 1000 ASU Drive 359 | Lorman, MS 39096-7500
Phone: 601.877.6111 | Fax: 601.877.2975 | www.alcorn.edu

Made in the USA
Middletown, DE
30 June 2023